TRICKS
OF THE
TRADE
FOR KIDS

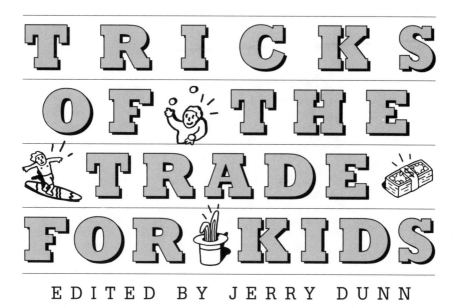

TRICKS OF THE TRADE FOR KIDS

EDITED BY JERRY DUNN

Houghton Mifflin Company
Boston ★ New York 1994

For information about permission to reproduce selections from this book,
write to Permissions, Houghton Mifflin Company, 215 Park Avenue South,
New York, New York 10003.

"How to Be a Success" by Mister Rogers, Judy Blume, Richard Dean
"MacGyver" Anderson, and Lee Iacocca copyright © Roosevelt Middle School.
"Win Big at Monopoly" by Philip Orbanes copyright © Philip E. Orbanes. "My
Thirteen Rules to Live By" by Colin Powell copyright © Colin Powell. "Make
the Very Best of Your Life" by Ronald Reagan copyright © Ronald Reagan.
"Dealing with the Death of Your Pet" by Mister Rogers copyright © 1993
Family Communications, Inc. "Learn to Juggle the Easy Way" by Dave
Finnegan copyright © Oliver D. Finnegan III. "Take Great Vacation Photo-
graphs" by Jodi Cobb copyright © Jodi Cobb. "Knock-Knock Joke Quiz" from
"Be a Great Punster" by Richard Lederer from *Get Thee to a Punnery*, copyright ©1988 Richard Lederer. Reprinted with the permission of the author and
the publisher, Wyrick & Company. "How to Build Mighty Biceps" by Arnold
Schwarzenneger with Charles Gaines, from *Arnold's Fitness for Kids—Ages
11–14*, published by Doubleday.

Library of Congress Cataloging-in-Publication Data
Tricks of the trade for kids / edited by Jerry Dunn.
    p. cm.
   Includes index.
   ISBN 0-395-65027-5
   1. Amusements—Juvenile literature. 2. Hobbies—Juvenile literature.
[1. Amusements. 2. Hobbies.] I. Dunn, Jerry Camarillo.
GV1203.T66 1994   94-22264
790.1'922—dc20   CIP
                                                        AC

Instructional diagrams by Victor Paredes
Flip art illustrations by Tom Sito
Animated cartoon illustrations by Sergio Aragonés
Cover illustrations by Stephen Schudlich

Printed in the United States of America

Book club edition reprinted by special arrangement with Houghton Mifflin Company.

*Dedicated with love to
Lachie and Graham,
who came to my office and
interrupted my work on
this book again and again...
and again, and again,
and again...*

Thank goodness!

Table of Contents

Introduction

As a kid, it's your job to ask questions that no average bumbling parent could possibly answer. You must also pester your mom and dad for help on impossible projects: "Mom, will you help me build the Eiffel Tower out of toothpicks?" "Hey, Dad! Teach me to tail a crook the way an FBI agent does!"

Your parents may be totally useless when it comes to these things, however, like the father of my two boys. (Oops, that's me!) This book can be your teacher. It's chock full of the "real work." That's the term magicians use for the inside tips that make a trick work perfectly.

If you want to draw animated cartoons, for instance, an artist from Walt Disney Studios will show you the real work on making a flip book. As a special bonus, there's a flip book built right into this book! If you want to build big biceps, take a lesson from Arnold Schwarzenegger. Want to make a lot of money with your own business? Ask Mrs. Fields (of cookie fame) for her trade secrets—and a favorite recipe. They're all here!

Tricks of the Trade for Kids will also show you how to win big at Monopoly, read minds, twirl a baton, get yourself in the *Guinness Book of World Records,* ride a surfboard like a pro, collect Barbie dolls for fun and profit, steal a base, fold a dollar bill into a finger ring, take vacation photos like a *National Geographic* photographer, and build an entire sandcastle city.

Here's a tip, though: Don't show this book to your parents. They'll wonder how you got so smart all of a sudden.

Let's just let that be our little secret.

How to Draw an Animated Flip Book like a Walt Disney Artist

by Tom Sito

H ave you ever been so bored in class that you took your notebook and did a different drawing in the corner of each page, and then flipped the pages to see your pictures move? (I used to draw two rocket ships smashing into each other with puffs of smoke.) That's basically animation, and it doesn't get much more complicated.

What you made was a "flip book," a great way to learn the ABC's of animated cartoons. A flip book is just a series of drawings creating the illusion that things are moving. It's the same principle I used to make the fish sing in *The Little Mermaid* or to make Roger Rabbit's eyes go *boinnnggggg.*

To create a flip book, you don't need any more advanced technology than a pen and a 3"x 5" scratch pad. Use a pad that's glued at one end (not a spiral notebook, which is too loose and jiggles around). Put a heavy clip at the glued end, so the pages won't move or fall out. Start drawing on the bottom piece of paper, and work forward (or, as animators say, "straight ahead"). The paper should be thin enough to see through; this allows you to use your last picture as a guide to draw the next one. (A black felt-tip pen shows up well.) After you have fifteen or twenty drawings, go back, hold the edge of the pad, and flip the pages.

The basic theory of animation is simple: The more drawings you do, the slower the action will be, and the fewer

As an animator at Walt Disney Studios, Tom Sito's screen credits include *Who Framed Roger Rabbit?* ("I killed the weasels," he says), *The Little Mermaid, Beauty and the Beast,* and *Aladdin.* President of the Motion Picture Screen Cartoonists Union, he has also worked on animated commercials and Saturday morning cartoons in New York, London, and Los Angeles. His specialty is wacky comedy and slapstick.

drawings, the faster the action. Let's say you want to draw Felix the Cat throwing a punch. He winds up his fist slowly, so you draw a lot of pictures, each one slightly different from the one before. But when he throws the punch, his hand moves fast and you need only one or two drawings. POW!

I've drawn a few samples, showing you how to make things and people seem to move—what we call "effects animation" and "character animation."

Bouncing ball

All animators start their careers with the bouncing ball. It's like "See Dick run." The bouncing ball demonstrates a principle we call "squash and stretch": As cartoon figures move, they can either condense (squash) or elongate (stretch) as a result of their action. In this example, a ball comes down, hits the ground, and squashes to a pancake shape. This may look exaggerated, but it's exactly what you see in a high-speed photograph of a basketball hitting the floor. "Squash and stretch" applies to bodies, too. Once I saw a film that showed the kind of pressure joggers put on their feet as they run. It was amazing—their feet looked like Daffy Duck's. So remember that human beings aren't rigid suits of armor; we're like mooshy bags—we squash and stretch.

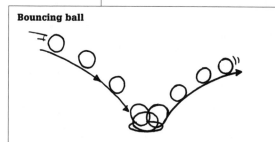

Bouncing ball

The bouncing ball also gives you a chance to experiment with timing. How rapidly is the ball coming down? How long does it delay on the ground before it pops up? These things are determined partly by how many drawings you do. Nobody can teach you timing, but you'll learn with experience.

Soap bubble

You are creating your own universe, so you can decide what's going on. This drawing could be a soap bubble, or maybe it's mud bubbling in a hot sulfur spring, like at Yellowstone Park. Mud bubbles up and pops slowly because it's dense, while a soap bubble is thinner and pops faster. (In general, water moves faster than you'd think. Be careful not to do too many drawings, or your water will look like ketchup or taffy.)

Soap bubble

In the drawing that comes right before the "pop," notice that the bubble actually implodes, or gets smaller. This gives a little more punch to the explosion. For some reason it's not as satisfying to go from the full shape to the burst; you need some of what animators call "antic," to create anticipation.

Rocket ship

Be sure not to draw the "speed lines" all the same length and in the same position, or the rushing rocket will look as if it's trailing a bunch of spaghetti. Speed lines should look a little different in each picture. But always keep them moving backwards, to show the direction of motion.

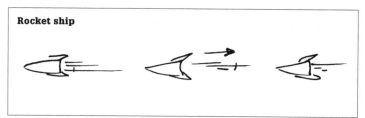

Rocket ship

H-bomb

An H-bomb might not be the most appropriate example, but what the heck—there's a bit of an anarchist in each of us!

The use of a white frame and a black frame is an old film device. The white is like a flash of blinding light, to which the black adds more impact. (Even live-action movies use this trick to make an explosion seem more dramatic.) Shock waves appear next, and then the smoke, which builds from the bottom. The column of smoke keeps feeding rapidly inside the mushroom cloud; the upper part of the cloud builds slowly. If you watch smoke, you'll see that it rolls in on itself as it expands.

H-bomb

Running man

The human body moves up and down as you run, and you can trace this movement as a wavy line—a series of curves, or "arcs." (You'll also see arcs in the drawing of the bouncing ball.) All of our major body movements are arcs, too. Swing your arm, and your hand moves in a curved path. If you draw a series of pictures of this swing, stack them up, and then shine a strong light through them, you'll see that all the hands form a smoothly curved line—the arc. At least, they *should;* if the line isn't smooth, your animation will look choppy and unrealistic.

Running man

By the way, there's no saying that an artist can't break the rules. When Popeye walks, for instance, his body *never* goes up and down. But his shoulders do, which gives him a funny, strutting walk. This makes him look like Popeye and no one else. As you get better at drawing characters, try playing with their walks. Does the character go up on his toes? Does he take long steps or teeny ones? Does his foot snap forward or drag sluggishly? Every person's walk is different—it's like a signature!

This brings us to what animation is really all about — creating a personality for a character through movement. In *The Little Mermaid* I drew some scenes of Sebastian, the crab. He's sort of a Caribbean gentleman, and a singer and dancer; but he's also a bit on the stuffy side, because he's trying to be a courtier to the king. The funny part about him is that although he makes sweeping gestures with his claws and adopts a regal attitude with his facial expressions, his little tiny crab legs are always going *ticka-ticka-ticka-ticka*. It just creates a funny image. His movements show his personality.

Movement is fascinating, a never-ending study. You can watch birds fly, notice someone's lip trembling when he's angry, or observe a person's walk, and just lose yourself in it. To draw movements that seem to create a living character is the real magic of animation.

What Makes Cartoons Funny?

To make your flip book funny, let your mind go free and think, "What would be the most outrageous thing I can do here?" A problem is that people edit themselves and say, "Oh, we *can't* do that." Well, why not?

Tex Avery, a great animation director at MGM Studios, used to hold "Oh no sessions," during which the artists would sit around and talk about what the cartoon characters might do next. They'd invent all kinds of gags, and eventually the conversation would get so tasteless and off the wall that someone would say, "Oh, no!" That's when Tex Avery would nod and say, "That's it! Put it in the picture."

There are standard gags that always seem to make people laugh. Once at Disney we did a film where Pegleg Pete gets his trousers cut and you see his underwear. Little kids go nuts if you show them underwear. They just howl. It always works.

The Art of Animation

Animation goes back to the stone age, when primitive men drew animals on a cave wall in Lascaux, France. They gave each animal six or eight feet, because they were trying to describe movement; the animals were running. In the same way, an animated cartoon exaggerates reality through movement.

Creating an animated feature such as *Beauty and the Beast* takes about five hundred people, of whom forty are master animators, helped by assistants. (I started out at Disney Studios animating on *Who Framed Roger Rabbit?*) In animation there's a lot of trial and error. One master animator used to say: "Your garbage can is your best friend. If it doesn't work, throw it out." That's how you learn.

An animated feature starts with a storyboard—a string of little visual sketches for each important scene in the story, showing how the picture works. It's like a blueprint of the film. There are many scenes, and in each one the characters will go through a sequence of positions called "major poses." Let's say that Roger Rabbit stands up from the table, turns, and walks out. The major poses will be Roger in his chair, Roger standing up, the pivot on the heel, and the exit. These are the landmark body positions. The animator draws them, and then his assistants draw the "in-betweens," the drawings that fill in between the main poses.

If you reduce a moving character to a stick figure, you'll see one basic line, and this "line of action" should show clearly what the character is thinking or doing. Let's imagine that Yosemite Sam says to Bugs Bunny: "You! Get out of here!" His gestures have to be clear by themselves, even without words: "You!" (Yosemite Sam points to Bugs.) "Get out of here!" (Yosemite Sam jerks his thumb toward the door.) That's an example of getting the line of action correct.

It helps to take the part of your character, like an actor in a play. Every Disney animator has a mirror on the side of their desk. If you came into my office, you'd find me making faces in the mirror, or maybe moving around the room and acting things out to myself. Like actors, animators build up a little library of memo-ries and sense impressions. In *Beauty and the Beast,* for example, I animated the scene where Beast is learning to eat with a spoon. He lifts the spoon and tries to get his head under it, so the food doesn't spill, and then he starts licking. In my mind, I remembered what a cat looks like drinking from a faucet. He sticks his head underneath and tries to lick. Basically, that's what Beast is doing—he's a cat under a faucet.

Animated characters have to interact and work off of each other, just like actors on a stage. There is an old actors' exercise based on a Laurel and Hardy comedy routine. If I pretend to spit in your eye, you have to look like you're getting it in the eye. Then you have to take it and throw it on my necktie, and I have to take it and throw it on your shoe. It's a back-and-forth kind of thing. Likewise, in animation your characters have to interact with each other. If one is talking, the other is *listening;* he's not just frozen, staring into space.

It's these little physical things that make cartoon characters seem to be human, and this is what makes animation so appealing. In *The Little Mermaid,* when Ariel's father is hollering at her, she bites her lower lip because she's so angry that she wants to yell. The simple gesture of biting her lip is so universal that it speaks to us.

What we do at Disney Studios is called "personality animation," and it's difficult because you are creating a *being.* Ariel the mermaid may be completely made up, but she exists now, independent of the movie. We believe her, just like we believe Bugs Bunny or Pinocchio. They all exist! That's great animation.

Sing like a Rock Star

by Seth Riggs

In my work as a vocal coach for top stars, I use some basic ideas I've developed to help anyone sing better. The same ideas can help *you* become a better singer, whether you want to sing rock 'n' roll or opera, musical comedy or reggae.

The main secret is simple: Singing is nothing more than sustained (drawn out) talking. You don't have to strain or do anything unnatural, like wrinkle your forehead, stand on your tiptoes, raise your shoulders, or stretch out your arms. Just be as natural as when you're talking. If you say "one-two-three-four-five" and then sing "one-two-three-four-five," you should do pretty much the same thing both times.

Find your natural singing range

Singing is as easy as talking only when you sing in a comfortable range for *your* voice. Your entire range is the spread from the lowest to the highest note you can sing. The most comfortable part of that range is close to where you talk. (That is, unless you talk in an exaggerated higher pitch like Michael Jackson, who raises his voice higher than his natural speech level.) To find this comfortable range, say "Hi, how are you?" in your regular voice. That's the range where you should start singing.

Never strain or change your posture trying to sing high notes. (After all, if standing on tiptoes helped you hit a high note, you could stand on a ladder and really get up there.) In-

The teacher of ninety Grammy winners, Seth Riggs coached Michael Jackson for the best-selling album of all time, *Thriller*, and accompanied him on the Bad Tour. His students also include opera stars, Stevie Wonder, Shanice Wilson, Bette Midler, Tevin Campbell, and Whoopi Goldberg. He teaches his methods in a book-and-tape/disc set called *Singing for the Stars* and in his videotape, *Singing with Seth*.

stead, stay physically relaxed, don't push your voice, and sing in the range that's easy for you.

Sing in tune

What if you can't carry a tune consistently? Practice! Sit down with a piano or guitar and play random notes within your most comfortable range. Try to match these notes with your voice, using sounds like *oooh* or *eeeh*. With some work, you'll be able to stay on pitch. (If you have trouble telling if you're matching your voice to the piano, use a tape recorder and play it back.)

A Great (but Silly) Way to Warm Up Your Voice

1. Do a trill. One way is to roll the tip of your tongue against your upper palate (the roof of your mouth, just behind your front teeth). Pretend it's cold outside and you're saying, "B-R-r-r-r-r-r." Or say "T-R-r-r-r-u-c-k." If you can't trill your tongue, make a sound with your lips like a motorboat: "B-B-b-b-b-b-b-b-b." As you do the trill, your voice can make a sound at some comfortable pitch.

2. Slide the pitch of your trill smoothly up and down. It sounds like a siren rising and falling. (Remember, the *loudness* of your voice doesn't rise and fall, only the *pitch.*) As you trill, extend the pitch as high and as low as you can without straining your vocal cords.

This simple exercise helps you hit many different pitches up and down the scale. And singing a trill is so totally silly that you won't get discouraged and think, "Oh gee, I'm not doing it like Michael Jackson or Natalie Cole." You're just warming up your voice with a funny exercise. By the way, if you prefer to practice the trill in private, you can do it in your room with the door closed. That way the men in the white coats won't come and take you away!

Another good idea is to sing along with the radio or a recording by someone whose voice is in the same range as yours. You'll know that a singer is in your range when you don't have to strain or push your voice to hit the notes.

Keep your Adam's apple down

As you sing, gently place your finger on your Adam's apple (your larynx, or voice box). You don't want it to move up, as it does when you swallow. If it rises, it will block off the steady stream of air that should flow out of your mouth as you sing. You'll feel choked and strained. (It's okay if your Adam's apple moves slightly as you sing the words to a song, but you don't want it to rise dramatically.)

Another trick: Don't smile while you sing, thinking it will make your voice sound brighter. It raises your larynx and tightens your throat. You should look conversational when you sing—as if you're talking to someone. Also avoid gasping for breath, because that chokes off your voice. To breathe correctly, stand up straight but relaxed, and push out your tummy. You'll feel this push creating a vacuum (empty space) inside your chest, and air will just drop in naturally. You don't have to *take* a breath; it happens by itself. When you breathe this way, your throat seems to relax, too. One more secret for relaxing your throat is to turn your head from side to side as you sing.

Find your vibrato

Vibrato is the wavering in your voice that makes the pitches sound rich and full. Sing the line "Mary Had a Little Lamb" straight and flat, with no vibrato, and that's how it sounds... flat. This is the way small children sing, and it sounds like yelling. But if you sing the line with vibrato, it sounds like a singer. To find your vibrato, sing and sustain the word "she." Sing it on a scale moving downward. (The notes would be *so fa mi re do*, which you can play on a piano and match with your voice.) As you sing, look for a little shake in your voice. That wavering is what you want to encourage.

Here's how to develop it: On a piano, play up and down the first five notes of the scale (*do re mi fa so*). Sing along, saying the syllable "ghee." Give it a little sob each time, crying up and down the scale. That should kick off some vibrato. I teach this exercise to the most sophisticated singers in the world, and it really works.

Practice all this, and you'll start to sound like a real singer yourself!

Betcha Can'ts

by Harry Anderson

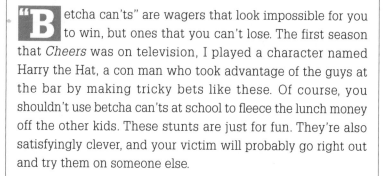**B**etcha can'ts" are wagers that look impossible for you to win, but ones that you can't lose. The first season that *Cheers* was on television, I played a character named Harry the Hat, a con man who took advantage of the guys at the bar by making tricky bets like these. Of course, you shouldn't use betcha can'ts at school to fleece the lunch money off the other kids. These stunts are just for fun. They're also satisfyingly clever, and your victim will probably go right out and try them on someone else.

Harry Anderson, who starred in TV's long-running "Night Court" and in "Dave's World," is the author of *Games You Can't Lose*. He has a son, Dashiell, age 7, and a daughter, Eva, 12. As an expert on tricky bets, he claims, "I've made plenty of money off my kids!"

You Do As I Do

You and a friend each pick up a glass with something in it to drink. You say, "Betcha can't do what I do." You raise your glass; he raises his glass. You hold your glass way over to one side; he does the same. You lift your glass over your head; he lifts his glass over his head. You drink what's in your glass; so does he. Now comes the twist: You spit your drink back into the glass — but he has *swallowed* his, thinking that that's what you did. You win the bet! This stunt is funny in front of an audience, so I do it at comedy clubs with a volunteer from the crowd, and the ending comes as a complete surprise.

Newspaper Fooler

This is an old trick. You say to a friend, "I bet that if I stand on one end of a sheet of newspaper and you stand on the other end, you won't be able to touch me." When he accepts your bet, lay the newspaper in an open doorway, stand on one side, and close the door between you. You win. Now offer to give your friend a chance to get even by making the same bet with you. Just make sure you're standing on the outside of the house when he shuts the door. By the time he says, "Okay, I win," you're long gone!

Paper-Tearing Challenge

Take a sheet of paper (notebook paper is fine) and make two parallel rips, tearing from one end nearly to the other end. You'll have three strips hanging from a half-inch strand. Bet your friend that he can't hold two of the ends, one in each hand, and tear the paper into three separate pieces with just one tug. It can't be done; the most he'll do is tear off one piece. When it's your turn, hold the two outside ends, lift the whole paper, and grip the center strip in your lips. Now tug with both hands, pulling off the other two strips. You end up with three pieces. You win again!

I'm Wrong

Here's a stunt that worked well on *Cheers*. Harry the Hat sat at the bar with a coin in his hand, and Norm asked what he was doing. Harry was holding up the coin and seemingly trying to find a position in the air for it. He said, "Well, if I find just the right place to put this coin, I can let go of it and it will stay suspended, floating in air." Norm answered, "You can't do that!"

"Okay," said Harry, "will you buy me a beer if I'm wrong?" When Norm agreed, Harry let go of the coin and it fell. "Well, I'm wrong," he said. "You owe me a beer." Remember that Harry the Hat had carefully used the word *wrong*.

This tricky bet will fool your friends, too, especially if you've already tried some of the earlier stunts, which set up a pattern. Then you can glide the tricky phrasing ("If I'm wrong...") right past people.

If you try this bet, you might say, "Will you give me a nickel if I'm wrong?" But really, you don't want to win money from your friends with these stunts. First, it's not nice to clip friends that way. And second, you run the risk that they've read this book, too—and that they'll win *your* money!

Fix Your Bike on the Road— without Tools

by Richard Ballantine

Richard Ballantine is the world's best-selling bicycle author. *Richard's Bicycle Book* has sold more than one million copies. His new *Richards' Ultimate Bicycle Book,* coauthored with Richard Grant, has already sold 100,000 copies in six languages. He was part of the Bluebell team, which in 1982 held the world speed record for bicycles.

 ou're out riding your bike, and something goes *pop*—a tire, a snapped cable—but you have no spare parts or tools. Don't worry. Most things can be fixed with whatever's on hand, plus a little imagination.

Puncture

What if a tire goes flat, and you haven't got a tube repair kit? Stuff things inside the tire to help give it some shape. You can use just about anything to "inflate" a tire this way. Try grass or leaves. Rummage around in a rubbish bin for old clothes or bits of foam or newspapers. Pack the material into the tire as tightly as possible.

Of course, if you're going to ride a bicycle with this kind of improvised tire, you should go slowly. Above all, don't ride fast around corners, because the tire could roll right off the rim. This is a trick to get you home.

Broken chain

If your chain breaks because a link pin falls out, you can repair it temporarily with a twig or a piece of wire or string.

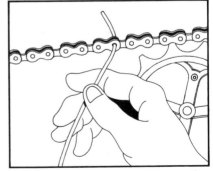

(When you're out in the countryside, look for the kind of twine that's used for tying up hay bales. It's unbelievably strong.) Insert the string or wire through the link holes. This will hold the links in place. Then wrap a piece of tape around the chain. (The teeth of the cog will punch holes in the tape as you ride). Pedal gently. If you suddenly stand on the pedals, the chain will come apart. Remember, you're just trying to limp home.

Broken cables

Two different kinds of problem can occur. If the cable for changing the gear breaks, and it breaks somewhere toward the handlebars, there's a pos-sibility of tying it to the frame or some other part of the bicycle. As you may know, if a derailleur gear hasn't got a cable on it, spring tension will carry it out to a very high gear. This makes it rather un-comfortable to pedal if you've got hills to climb. In this situation pull the broken cable tight, so that the derailleur moves to a lower gear. Wrap the cable around, let's say, the seat tube. Tie it in place. Away you go, pedaling in a gear that's much easier.

If the brake cable snaps, you'll need to bridge the distance between the two frayed cable ends. So find something, any-thing, that will serve the purpose. It may be a stick that's about a foot or two long. Tie the broken ends of the cable to either end of the stick. Or you can use the shoelace from your shoe. If you're really stuck, tear off a piece of your shirt! In a pinch I once used a flattened tin can, punching holes in each end and tying the cable ends through them.

Loose bolt or nut

It's not hard to make an improvised wrench. Tie a piece of string around one end of a stick, preferably a flat-sided one.

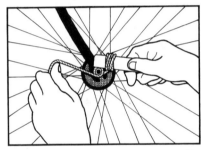

Wrap the other end of the string around the nut several times, until it's got a good grip. Then use the stick like a wrench handle, to give yourself the leverage to tighten the nut (or loosen it, as the case may be). This technique sounds desperate, but it works very well.

As you can see, getting out of these ticklish situations is as much a matter of having a "can do" attitude as anything else. Look around for whatever material is at hand, and use your most important tool—your ingenuity.

Coping with the Death of Your Pet

by Mister Rogers

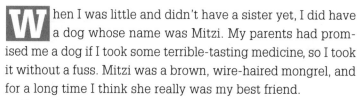hen I was little and didn't have a sister yet, I did have a dog whose name was Mitzi. My parents had promised me a dog if I took some terrible-tasting medicine, so I took it without a fuss. Mitzi was a brown, wire-haired mongrel, and for a long time I think she really was my best friend.

In each other's company, we learned a lot about the world. We explored our neighborhood and beyond, and I remember feeling a little braver when Mitzi was with me. We shared times of excitement, joy, and sorrow. When Mitzi died, I was very sad. For a long time afterwards I played with a stuffed toy dog, pretending it would die and then come back to life. Only little by little did I stop playing out that drama.

It can be frightening when pets, as they will, have accidents, get ill, grow old, or die. I think these difficult times help us learn that a great many sad things happen in life that we aren't able to prevent and of which we are not the cause. The death of a pet means that we must confront one of the hard facts of life—that all living things eventually die. This remains difficult for many of us to face, all of our lives.

Your parents can give you a lot of help understanding death. A friend of mine told me not long ago about a little boy who buried one of his pet fish and seemed to understand that it was dead. Several days later, though, peering at the fishes that remained in the tank, he asked his mother, "Which is the one that died?" His mother had the chance, again, to talk with him

Mister Rogers is the host of television's longest-running children's program, "Mister Rogers' Neighborhood." He has received countless awards, been spoofed by the likes of Eddie Murphy, and dedicated his life to encouraging the healthy emotional growth of children.

about death. The more we talk about things, the better we can understand them and manage them.

When a loved family pet does die, it can also be a time to see that strength can be communicated through tears. I know a man who had to bring home the news to his children that their beloved dog had been killed. He cried and the children cried, and they were able to comfort each other. Seeing their father openly express his grief let them know that it's all right for boys and men to cry, just as it's all right for girls and women. It's human to have and to express a wide range of feelings.

Allowing time for the family to grieve before getting a new pet is important in the healing process. Sometimes many weeks go by before a family is ready for a new pet. And that time can be used to deal with the natural feelings of loss of the past as well as to begin to feel enthusiasm for the future.

My children raised a succession of pets, and perhaps it was in watching them do so that I began to realize what Mitzi had meant to me. My younger son, John, had a dachshund named Frisky who would sleep on his bed. At night my wife and I could hear John telling Frisky all his troubles. Years ago Frisky died after a full life, and that sad time made me think of all the growing up we had done together.

No doubt, in time, John will have another dog. I hope he will, for his sake and for the dog's. Animals must sense who really loves them. Perhaps someday one of John's pets will help *his* children grow, just as I believe Mitzi helped me.

The Art of Performing Magic
by Harry Blackstone, Jr.

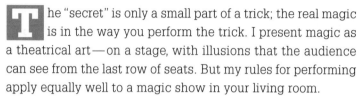

he "secret" is only a small part of a trick; the real magic is in the way you perform the trick. I present magic as a theatrical art—on a stage, with illusions that the audience can see from the last row of seats. But my rules for performing apply equally well to a magic show in your living room.

Properly performed, magic is an art. Like painting or poetry, it expresses ideas that lie deep in human experience. Making someone disappear and then reappear in a different place, for instance, has something to do with the age-old dream of being able to "wish ourselves" to a different location.

A great magician works with the question "What if?" He (or she) takes the everyday world and stretches its limits. In doing a trick—let's say, shredding a sheet of newspaper and then restoring it—he shows the audience something that is considered impossible. If he performs well, he creates an encounter with the mysterious, and, most of all, he entertains his audience. Here's how to perform that kind of magic yourself.

Make magic fun

Magic should be presented in a pleasing way. Beginning performers, however, tend to adopt an attitude: "Here's a trick I can do but you can't, so I'm going to *fool* you." Audiences don't want to be fooled; they want to be entertained. (And they certainly don't want to be made fools of.) Develop a warm relationship with your audience.

Harry Blackstone, Jr., made his first stage appearance—and disappearance—at the age of six months, during the magic show presented by his father, The Great Blackstone. Today his own show, blending the classics of magic and modern illusions, has received rave reviews on Broadway and continues to tour the world. Blackstone also appears on public television's "Square One TV," teaching mathematics to young people through magic.

Develop each trick into a story

A good magician is like a storyteller, so I try to weave tricks into stories. For example, I became interested in an illusion invented many years ago—that of pushing objects through a sheet of solid glass. Before adding it to my evening show, however, I needed to create a story around the trick. By luck I was able to buy an actual window used in the film of *The Wizard of Oz*, and that window gave me an idea. On-stage I tell the story of Dorothy sitting in her room as the tornado comes closer. She's looking through the window, which is a single sheet of glass, crisscrossed by strips of wood to make four panes. To protect the glass, Dorothy places a shutter over each pane. Each shutter has a round hole, which I tell the audience could be dangerous because of flying objects during a tornado. "The wind can drive a piece of straw right into a tree! The same goes for a steel rod." I pick up a rod with a long ribbon trailing from it, and I push it through a pane of glass. There's no damage. After threading the rod and ribbon through every pane, I lift the glass out of the frame. It's still in one piece! To end my story, Dorothy magically appears on stage. Then she passes through a big sheet of glass, and the audience actually watches her go.

The Magician's Code of Honor

Never tell the secret! Revealing the secret destroys the mystery and magic. People will feel that your miracle was just a cheap trick.

Never repeat a trick for the same audience! They might figure out the trick if they get a second chance to see it. And since they know what to expect, they might catch you doing the "dirty work."

In this way I took an old trick and transformed it into a story about *The Wizard of Oz,* a tale everyone loves. Instead of being just a trick, it's now a lovely piece of fantasy.

Remember that you—not your props— create the magic

Beginning magicians often make the mistake of letting their props get between themselves and their audience. Magic props are clever and fun, but they are called "props" because they *support* the performance. You mustn't get overly involved with the apparatus, or you become just a demonstrator of the equipment, not a performer of *magic*. (If that's what audiences wanted, they would go to a magic shop.) Instead, you must entertain them, which you do with your own personality, not with boxes and trick devices.

Look at your audience

Work to one member of the audience at a time, and *make eye contact*. Then move on and look at another person, and another. Don't gaze over their heads, as if you were a politician giving a speech. Communicate with your audience as individuals—a group of ones, not one group.

Treat your volunteers properly

When you need volunteers for a trick, look for people whom your intuition tells you will be cooperative and fun. They may be a little nervous, so you can sometimes ask your audience to

encourage them to come on-stage. If they *really* don't want to be in the spotlight, don't force or embarrass them into volunteering. Just move on to someone else.

Once volunteers are on-stage, treat them with respect. You can have fun with them, but never make them the butt of a joke.

Rehearse thoroughly

Practice the mechanical moves of your trick until they are second nature, until you don't even have to look at your hands or the prop. Also, plan out the words you'll say—what magicians call "patter." Eventually, you'll be ready to perform the trick for an audience. And the only way to rehearse a performance is to go out there and perform.

Routine your show

Let's say you have a bunch of tricks that you learned from books or bought at the magic shop. How do you turn them into a show? One rule is never to repeat an effect in the same performance. If every trick involved the appearance of silk handkerchiefs, it would quickly get boring.

Your opening trick must accomplish two things—catching the audience's eye and establishing your credentials as a magician. My own opening trick is the Vanishing Bird Cage, the perfect example of the old magical saying, "Now you see it; now you don't." I step on-stage holding a bird cage with a canary in it. I introduce myself, say that I'm a magician, and *boom*—the whole cage and canary disappear!

Then it's time to establish your personality with the audience. I do this by inviting children to come up while I get another cage and canary to do the trick again. My personality comes out as I joke with the kids.

It's a plus if your show has continuity, some thread to tie it together from beginning to end. In my show there's a Merlin character who comes on-stage while I'm asking kids to help with the second bird cage vanish. I say, "No, I asked for *little* people." He crouches down, but I chase him off the stage. A couple more times during the show, he interrupts me and I have to send him away. At the end of the show, Merlin comes out with a gun. I pick up a piece of cloth, and he shoots into it. The cloth drops, and I've turned into a gorilla. Now he fires at the gorilla, the head comes off, and it turns out to be one of the young assistants in my show. For the climax, Old Merlin takes off his outfit—and it's yours truly! The continuity runs from the first trick of my show to the last. The audience expects Merlin to behave in one way, and he does—up to the point of the final surprise.

Place your greatest piece of entertainment in the *second-to-last* position. Exactly what trick you do depends on your performing style and personality. If you present yourself as a mysterious character, for instance, then your most mystifying effect comes here. Given my style, I do a comedy pickpocket routine in which I invite men on-stage and then proceed to steal things from them, even though my hands are tied behind me—their

Three Miracles You Can Do

The Banana Miracle

Here's a magical moment you can create at the kitchen table.

Effect: You show your audience a banana. Then you pick up a butter knife and use it like a magic wand to tap the fruit. "This is how I make my breakfast…with magic," you say. "Please peel the banana." When the peel is removed, the banana is seen to be magically sliced!

Secret: Ahead of time, get a banana and a sewing needle. About one-third of the way from one end of the banana, poke the needle through the banana peel. Carefully push the needle through the soft inside of the banana, but *not* through the other side of the peel. Move the needle back and forth across the inside of the banana, until the banana is sliced clear through. Then carefully remove the needle from the hole you poked it through. Do this again about two-thirds of the way down the banana.

When your friend peels the banana, it will be mysteriously sliced into three parts—a miracle!

The Lie Detector Miracle

Effect: Someone picks a card from a deck, remembers it, and puts it back. You call out the names of the suits (hearts, clubs, spades, diamonds) and numbers (ace through king). Each time, your friend is to say whether you're right or wrong. She can tell the truth or lie. At the end you say, "I could tell when you lied." To prove it, you name the exact card she chose!

Secret: Ahead of time, separate the black cards from the red cards. Put the reds on top of the blacks.

Hold the deck with faces down. Fan the cards—but only the top half. Your friend doesn't know it, but she has to choose a red card. While she is looking at it and remembering it, square up the deck again. Then fan the bottom half. She replaces her card in that portion. Now announce that you'll find her card. Look through the faces of the cards (but don't let her see them). The red card she chose will be very easy to spot among the blacks. Remember it!

"Hmmm...I can't seem to find your card," you say innocently. Shuffle the deck. (This sneakily destroys the evidence!) Tell your friend, "I'm going to name the four suits, and then the numbers. For each one, you must answer yes or no. It doesn't matter if you tell the truth or lie. I can always tell!" When you've finished, announce the name of the chosen card (which you knew the whole time). Perform this trick with a bit of showmanship, and you've got a miracle on your hands!

Miracle of the Magic Dust

Effect: From a small box you remove some "magic dust" and rub it on the back of your friend's closed hand. When she opens her fist, some of the magic dust is now *inside* her hand! An unsolved mystery!

Secret: Ahead of time, take a small box and put some cooled-down ashes from the fireplace or an ashtray into it. Just before you do the trick, lick the tip of the middle finger on your right hand, and dip it into the ashes. Some of the ash will stick to your finger. To conceal the ash, bend your fingers toward the palm of your hand.

Ask your friend to hold out her left hand, with the palm facing down. Take it with your right hand and say, "Hold it a little lower," as you move it downward a few inches. While you do this, press your middle finger against her palm. Some of the ash will be left there. Without pausing, say, "Okay, close your hand into a fist."

The sneaky part of the trick is over. Now you can build it up. Take out the box, and display the magic dust. Dip your right middle finger into the box, where it will pick up a little of the ash. Rub it on the back of her closed left hand. The ash will disappear into her skin. Say some magic words. By now your friend won't remember that you touched her hand earlier. When she opens her fingers and sees the ash on her palm, she just won't believe it. Another marvel!

watches, their wallets, and finally a necktie and shirt right off one man's back!

To end your performance, use some kind of "flash" effect. (In my show, it's the Merlin exchange.) This last trick should be something that leaves the audience wanting more, but satisfied with a good performance.

Don't try to perform every trick you know

Once a boy went up to a great magician and said, "I can do a hundred tricks!" The master, who had traveled all over the world with his magic, said, "That's wonderful; I can do only ten." But he performed those ten tricks better than anybody else on earth. The point is, don't try to learn a thousand routines; learn a few tricks perfectly, and build your act around the strongest ones. Carry on the great traditions of magic as a theatrical art form.

Collect Barbie Dolls for Fun— and Profit

by Evelyn Burkhalter

The most popular doll in the history of the world has also become one of the favorite "collectibles." I think it's because you don't have to be wealthy to be a collector, just an average person. Over the years I accumulated so many Barbies that I opened a museum, the Barbie Hall of Fame, to exhibit about 10,500 Barbies and her friends, their clothes, cars, and other items.

Barbie fascinates me because, for the past thirty years, she's been a mirror of ordinary American life. The couple who created Barbie in 1959 owned the Mattel toy company, and they named the doll after their own daughter, Barbara (who was really embarrassed by the whole thing). Since then, Barbie has reflected the way we live, always changing with the times. When Jackie Kennedy was in the White House, Barbie had a similar bubble hairdo and wore hats and gloves. And when the Beatles came along and changed the way we dressed and talked, Barbie went mod with wild clothes and long hair. The new doll's knees could bend and her waist twist, for dancing to rock 'n' roll. During the civil rights movement, Mattel introduced a black Barbie. For the physical fitness boom of the 1980s, Barbie became an aerobics instructor. She's always in the mainstream of what's happening in America.

Barbie has had many careers—fashion designer, rock star, surgeon, business executive, jet pilot, TV personality, ballerina,

Evelyn Burkhalter has collected every Barbie and accessory made since 1959. A doll restorer and appraiser, she opened the Barbie Hall of Fame in 1984, which was Barbie's twenty-fifth anniversary year. She has appeared on national television as a Barbie expert.

and more—with lots of accessories, including hot tubs, airliners, and recording studios. And she's worn wonderful clothes, from formal gowns (created by fashion designers like Oscar de la Renta) to Malibu Beach bikinis to "Miss Astronaut" spacesuits.

It's no wonder that Barbies are such fun to collect. Here are some tips for starting and building your own collection.

New Barbies

Buy only dolls and outfits whose boxes say Limited Edition or Special Edition. Mattel makes only about 50,000 of each, so they're rarer and more collectible. (The company manufactures millions of the regular dolls and clothes, which have no collector's value at all.) About sixty limited editions are released each year; prices start at around $19, so you don't have to spend a lot of money, and they go as high as $365. Look for limited editions in doll stores and in catalogs from Sears, JCPenney, and FAO Schwarz. Each year Mattel puts out a special-edition Barbie made of porcelain, with clothes by designers like Bob Mackie (who creates outfits for Cher and other superstars), and a Holiday Barbie for Christmas.

Barbie's friends are also very collectible, especially her pals from different ethnic groups. Teresa is Hispanic; Christie is black; Kira is Asian. Not as many people buy these dolls, so they're rarer than regular Barbies. You may also want to collect the international dolls, which are dressed in beautiful costumes from different countries.

If you're collecting for future value, leave the dolls and outfits in their original boxes. Collectors refer to this condition as "NRFB" ("Never Removed From Box"). If you're just collecting for fun, though, take your Barbies out to display them. Barbie is much easier to see out of the box.

It's great to have one of Barbie's cars from the same time period as the doll, and (if you have room) one of her houses. The townhouse is a good one; it's not a new item, but Mattel keeps changing the background pictures as trends in home furnishings change. The townhouse is three stories tall and has an elevator that really works.

Buy regular Barbies (not the limited editions) to play with—that's what dolls are for!

Beware of Fakes!

Because original Barbie dolls and accessories have become so valuable to collectors, some dishonest people have learned to alter dolls so they appear rarer. There's a way to turn a #3 Barbie into a more valuable #2 by making certain changes in the doll, and these counterfeits sometimes appear for sale. There are also reproductions on the market. The original compact from Barbie's Roman Holiday outfit sells for as much as $800, for instance, so people make less expensive new replicas for collectors. Makers usually say that they're reproductions, but as the items pass from hand to hand, this little fact sometimes gets "forgotten," and eventually someone will try to sell it as an original. Be careful, and ask advice from more experienced collectors before you buy.

Older Barbies

The oldest and rarest doll is Barbie #1, made in 1959, and the price for a #1 NRFB has risen to $5,000. Mattel manufactured two blonde dolls for every brunette, so a Barbie #1 with brown hair is supposed to be rarer and is worth a little bit more.

But here's a tip: The trend now is toward collecting the second version (or "edition") of every Barbie. When the second edition comes out, a lot of people have already bought the first one, so they don't pay much attention. Because Mattel doesn't sell as many second editions, they are rarer. Today a #1 is still worth more, because it's the first example, but a #2 can be harder to find. If you have a #2 in your collection, it will grow in value.

Barbie's clothes are also great collectibles. One example is a little mink coat made exclusively for Sears in 1964 (it was the first special edition item in their catalog), and you couldn't touch it now for less than $2,500. (It's just a little piece of fur!) Among Barbie's early outfits, the most desirable collectibles are the Gay Parisienne, the Roman Holiday, and the Easter Parade, which were modeled on clothes in Audrey Hepburn movies. In their original boxes, they're worth about $1,500 per outfit.

Also valuable are the Jackie Kennedy fashions of 1965–67. (Collectors refer to them as the "1600s," because those were the Mattel catalog numbers.) They include pillbox hats, spiked high-heel shoes, and long, colored gloves. Apparently, Mattel was pushing other toys at the time and didn't make many of these outfits, so they're rare and valuable today. They were made very well; the dresses and coats even had linings. An NRFB outfit is worth $300 to $900. (Because of the expense, many collectors put together these ensembles piece by piece.)

Barbie's accessories are also fun to collect. She's been given just about everything a material girl could want—her own Chris-Craft yacht, a United airliner, a 1960s living room with Kingston Trio records on the floor, an Olympic ski village (with a ski jump), a swimming pool that has a slide and a working shower, and all kinds of cars, from a '57 Chevy convertible to a racy Ferrari.

How do you locate older Barbies, clothes, and accessories? Occasionally, you may get lucky and spot them at flea markets, garage sales, and thrift shops. That's the most fun. There are doll shows in just about every city, where dealers display, trade, and sell Barbies. Also, look in the local newspaper for classified ads placed by collectors with Barbies to sell.

When you get more serious about collecting, you should do some reading to broaden your knowledge. First, subscribe to *Barbie Bazaar* magazine (see "More about Barbie" on page 49 for information). It has articles on collectors and how they collected their Barbies. There's a classified ad section, and if you send the advertisers a self-addressed, stamped envelope, they will send you their lists of whatever is for sale. After you study a few lists, you'll have a better idea of prices all around the world, not just in your city or state.

One caution: These dealers are strangers to you, so you should check to make sure they're honest and reliable before buying from them. To find out about a dealer's reputation, you can talk to local Barbie collectors, phone the editors of *Barbie Bazaar* magazine, or call me at the Barbie Hall of Fame (see

Amazing Facts about Barbie

■ Ninety-five percent of American girls between the ages of three and eleven own at least one Barbie doll.

■ In its original box, a Barbie #1 is worth about 1,700 times what it sold for in 1959. Today, the price is about $5,000.

■ If Barbie were a real person, she would stand 5 feet, 6 inches tall, with measurements of 39-18-33. Her dress would be a size 7, her weight 110 pounds.

■ Mattel is the world's largest doll clothing maker, selling 20 million Barbie fashions annually. Mattel seamstresses can make two bouffant skirts and twenty bodices for Barbie gowns from only an eighth of a yard of fabric. Over the years, her clothes have required 75 million yards of cloth.

■ During a search for someone to portray "Rocker Barbie," Mattel received photographs and demo tapes from 60,000 women, ranging from a seven-year-old girl to a seventy-year-old grandmother from Illinois.

■ Barbie has a last name. She is Barbie Millicent Roberts. The daughter of George and Margaret Roberts, she graduated from Willow High and then attended State College.

■ In honor of Barbie's twenty-fifth anniversary in 1984, Tiffany jewelers created a $50,000 Barbie made of sterling silver.

■ A Barbie doll is sold about every two seconds. With total sales of 600 million around the world, Barbie is the most successful toy ever created. Laid end to end, all these Barbies would circle the globe more than three times.

"More about Barbie"). Don't just plunge in. And be sure to get a written sales receipt stating exactly what the doll is supposed to be. That way you have a legal document to protect you.

You can learn about the markings on the backs of Barbies, which identify the years they came out, in a great sourcebook called *The Collectors' Encyclopedia of Barbie Dolls and Collectibles* by Sybil Dewein and Joan Ashabraner. It contains accurate information about Barbies from 1959 to 1976, and it's available through your public library.

You may want to start your collection with the international dolls and their foreign costumes; it's a great way to learn about geography. Or maybe you'll collect Barbie's family members, like little sister Skipper, which are smaller dolls. Or you might like Ken; the "Rocker" version with long hair is very popular.

Whatever dolls you collect, have a great time! The world of Barbie is fascinating and fun. Welcome to it!

More about Barbie

To see a display of more than 10,000 Barbie dolls, fashions, and accessories, visit:

The Barbie Hall of Fame
Evelyn Burkhalter, curator
433 Waverley Street
Palo Alto, CA 94301
Telephone: (415) 326-5841

To learn more about Barbie or Barbie doll collecting, you can read or subscribe to:

Barbie Bazaar
5617 6th Avenue
Kenosha, WI 53140
Telephone: (414) 658-1004
Magazine aimed at older collectors

Barbie, the Magazine for Girls
300 Madison Avenue
New York, NY 10017
Telephone: (212) 687-0680
Articles on Barbie, interests for girls

Make the Ultimate Peanut Butter Sandwich

by William F. Buckley, Jr.

William F. Buckley, Jr., founded the *National Review,* **a magazine that is the voice of the American conservative political movement. He is known for his witty control of the English language.**

I like my peanut butter on highly toasted dark bread with just a touch of honey on it. For breakfast, that to me is the *sine qua non,* which is Latin for "the one thing that is absolutely essential." It's the start of a good day.

The best peanut butter is made by a company called Red Wing. But it doesn't go under that label. It's sold under the label of whatever the local grocery story calls itself. So if the ABC Grocery ordered Red Wing, it would come as ABC Peanut Butter.

But here's a clue to help you find it: Red Wing peanut butter always has a yellow plastic top. So run, don't walk, to your nearest store and see if they have it. I've never found anybody who thought it was less than the very best they ever tasted.

Frisbee Magic

by Dan "Stork" Roddick

It all started back in the 1920s, when college students discovered how much fun it was to throw metal pie tins. These were made in Connecticut by the Frisbie Baking Company. In 1957, the Wham-O Company put a plastic flying disc into the toy stores. The rest is history: More than *one hundred million* Frisbee discs have been sold.

You can do fantastic things with this simple piece of plastic. But it's no fun to just hack away, watching helplessly as the Frisbee curves and smacks into the ground. To be good, you must know the secrets of the Frisbee masters. Here they are!

THE BASICS
Throwing a Frisbee straight

A lot of people pick up a Frisbee and say, "I can never throw one of these things; it always curves to the right and turns over." (Players call this a "roll curve," because when the disc hits the ground, it rolls on its edge.) To fix the problem, use the correct grip. Grasp the disc as if you were going to fan yourself with it. Your thumb is 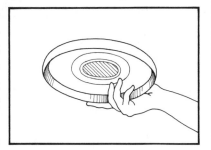 on top; your fingers are spread across the bottom, except your index finger, which curls along the outside of the rim. How

A member of the Frisbee Hall of Fame and past president of the World Flying Disc Federation, Dan Roddick is director of sports promotion for Wham-O. He has been the world flying disc champion in accuracy and freestyle and was twice the World Senior Overall Champion. He threw his first wobbly flight in 1953.

tightly should you grip the disc? Imagine you are holding a canary. You don't want it to get away, but you don't want to kill it either.

You also have to let go of the disc correctly. Tilt the disc so that the edge opposite your hand angles toward the ground. (For you geometry students, the disc is no longer parallel to the ground, but at about a 60-degree angle.) Frisbee pros call this tilt "hyzer." When you throw, release the disc smoothly; otherwise, it may wobble and curve to the right.

Although it is a pretty magical thing, a Frisbee doesn't fly by sheer magic. If you throw it flat-handed, with no spin, it will flop through the air like an ugly duck. You have to give it lots of spin. Do this by snapping your wrist when you let go of the disc. Think of snapping a towel. (Since the main activity in all

physical education classes is rat-tailing towels in the locker room and snapping other kids on the bottom, you already know how to do this, just to survive.) Or imagine you have Jell-O on your fingertips. To get rid of it, you'd move your hand forward and then stop it quickly, hoping that the Jell-O would keep going.

It's the same way with a Frisbee. Move your hand forward, then suddenly stop your hand and release the disc. That gives it spin. It's not a matter of moving your arm fast; it's an actual snap of the wrist.

Stance is important, too. Make sure your feet are placed along the line of your planned flight, not across it. Now you can turn your upper body for full power release.

Then there's timing. If you're trying to throw a Frisbee to your partner but it keeps hitting the house, throw it a little earlier or a little later.

> ## Frisbee Contests
>
> **If you'd like to join 700,000 other youngsters competing in the championships organized each year by schools, parks, and recreation departments, write to:**
>
> **Junior Frisbee Disc Championships**
> **835 East El Monte Street**
> **San Gabriel, CA 91778**

Skipping a Frisbee

You can skip the Frisbee so it hits the ground and flies up to your partner. For this trick the disc has to hit the ground on the edge opposite to your hand. You'd think that if you want the nose to bounce up, then the nose should hit the ground. But the Frisbee will just skitter along the ground to your partner. When the edge (or wing) of the Frisbee hits the ground, how-

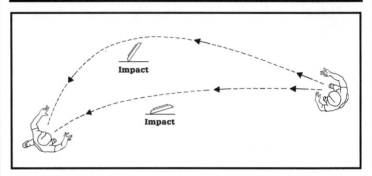

ever, the "bounce" transfers to the nose, bringing the nose up. (Weird, huh?) Since the disc has to be curving, you angle the edge of the disc downward as you release it, giving it lots of hyzer. Frisbee fans call this throw a "skip curve."

The correct skipping point on the ground is about halfway between you and your partner. As you get farther apart, though, you'll need to bounce it closer to your partner.

Boomerang throw

Making the Frisbee come back to you is the perfect game for people who have no friends. (Well, at least none available…) The first time you'll probably fling the disc high into the wind, and it will turn over and blow back over your head. To fix this little problem, tilt the edge of the disc downward (more hyzer), and throw with a strong wrist snap.

With a right-handed backhand throw, if the disc has a *lot* of tilt, it tends to curve left and then come sliding back down on the wind, too fast to catch. Instead, you want the disc to go up and float awhile, make a curve to the right, and come down slowly. (The "hang time" is measured as Maximum Time Aloft, or M.T.A., in a Frisbee contest.)

To get lots of hang time, do three things: Use a little less hyzer, keep the nose (front) of the Frisbee from pointing up too much as you release it, and throw the disc across the wind. (The illustration shows how to aim your Frisbee and what will happen if you throw it correctly.) Remember that the stronger the wind, the lower you should throw, because the wind can lift the disc and turn it over. Finally, here's an inside secret: Use a Fastback Frisbee, which you can find at Kmart. It's lighter, so it will float longer.

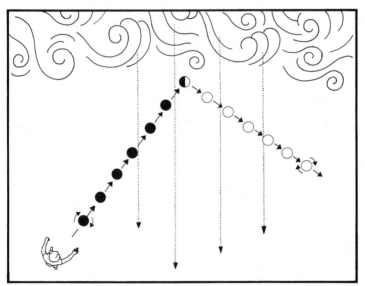

As the disc sails slowly down, you run over to your right and catch it. A perfect boomerang flight!

ADVANCED PLAY

When your partner tosses you a slow throw that hovers in the air, it's fun to catch it by having the Frisbee spin on your fingertip. This is called "delaying," the basic move of advanced Frisbee play. But first, let's learn two little tricks—"twirling" and "tipping"—to work our way up to delaying.

Twirling

Extend your index finger, curved just a little. As the floating Frisbee arrives, try to match the speed of the disc by moving either your hand or your whole body. (You may have to run along with the flying Frisbee or turn your body as it comes.) Be sure  to "give" with the disc; that is, lower your hand at the same speed as the disc is falling; otherwise, the Frisbee will hit your fingertip and bounce off.

When your index finger touches the bottom of the disc, the Frisbee will slide across your fingertip to the rim. When it does, pick up the spin by twirling your finger. The disc will revolve around your fingertip!

Tipping

The next step is to tap the bottom of the Frisbee to lift it in the air. First, take a magic marker and blacken the very center of the bottom as a target. As the Frisbee comes floating overhead, hold your middle finger straight, but not stiff. Give the Frisbee one sharp, quick tap in the middle. The disc will rise a couple of inches and come back down; now use your first finger for the twirl. Keep practicing until you can do several tips in a row before the twirl.

The bad news is that hitting the center won't work after four or five tips. The disc will start to angle away, out of control. You must learn to adjust the angle by tipping the disc off center. But where should you hit it? Follow this basic rule of physics: When you tip a disc, the effect is felt a quarter of the way farther around the Frisbee in the direction of the spin. For an example, look at the picture, which shows the bottom of a disc hovering above you. If the tail (section D) is too low, you tip the wing (section C). The lift will transfer to the tail, correcting the angle of the Frisbee so it spins flat in the air.

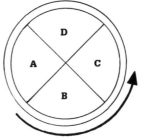

Now you can continue to tip the black spot in the center. Every time the disc starts to tilt and get slightly out of control, correct by tipping off center. And don't worry about having to think, "Let's see, where do I tip it?" You will soon be able to hit the right place automatically.

Delaying

The first two tricks, twirling and tipping, were just appetizers; here is the main course. The idea is to put your fingernail under the Frisbee and hold (or "delay") the spinning disc for a while. Slightly bend your forefinger, so the nail will be touching the plastic. (Your fingernail works well because it's more slippery than your fingertip.) If the Frisbee is floating above your eye level, hold your hand with the palm facing outward; if it's below eye level, turn your wrist so the palm faces toward you.

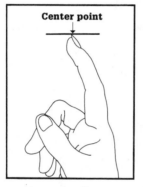

Center point

First, do one quick tip to make the Frisbee spin flat in the air, and let it settle on your fingernail. Now you're ready to delay, which is really just a continuous adjustment of the Frisbee as its spins on your fingertip. Since it's nearly impossible to keep your fingernail in the exact center, you move your hand in little circles, rotating in the direction of the spin. This corrects the Frisbee's angle from one instant to the next, so it spins flat. (Note: Beginners usually make fast, jerky circles, because they don't have good muscle control yet. It's like handwriting; at first, it's not easy to make smooth loops.) With practice, you'll be making small, slow circles, and the disc will spin easily on your fingernail.

Here's a hint: Delaying is easier if the Frisbee is slippery, so coat the bottom with silicon. A good brand is Krylon, sold in spray cans in the paint department at the hardware store. Spray lightly, including the rim, then use an old sock or something to wipe it off.

Once you can delay the disc for a while, try some advanced tricks. Let's say the disc is spinning on your right fingertip: You could pass it under your leg to your left hand, then bring it up,

Practicing Twirls, Tips, and Delays

You'll progress faster if you practice tossing the disc up in the air for yourself. (A friend might deliver only three or four properly hovering throws in a span of five minutes, but in that time you can toss fifty of them yourself, giving you a lot more practice.) You can do this in the comfort and convenience of your bedroom, which your mom will prefer to the living room, where there are things that can break.

Raise the disc over your head, as if it were coming down in a hovering flight. Hold one hand on each side, fingers pointed toward the ceiling. The plastic touches your fingers at the fingertip joints; your thumbs aren't involved. Bring the disc down to eye level, and twist your wrists; the right hand moves away from you, the left hand toward you. To spin the disc, raise it and untwist your wrists at the same time—it's a quick motion. Brush your hands in opposite directions as you loft the disc above your head. Now the Frisbee is spinning right above you. When it comes down, practice twirling, tipping, or delaying it.

roll it across your body to the right hand, delay it…and so on. It looks great—and it's all based on the building block of the delay!

Fun Frisbee Facts

■ More flying discs are sold each year than baseballs, basketballs, and footballs combined.

■ Wham-O's first disc was called the Pluto Platter. It was marketed in 1957, when Americans were fascinated by rumors of UFOs (Unidentified Flying Objects) from other planets.

■ A special vocabulary was developed by Frisbee fans in the 1950s. For example: "If a wrimpleplat misses the sprovit, it is blort, but it might fall with the vit and be a grunde." Translation: "When a disc is badly thrown onto the playing field, it will be out of bounds or it might fall short."

■ The world distance record for tossing a disc is 190.07 meters—more than the length of two football fields!

■ Virtually everyone in the United States has heard of the Frisbee, and nearly 90 percent of Americans have played with a flying disc.

How to Train a Frisbee Dog

by Peter Bloeme and Whirlin' Wizard

You've probably seen a dog race after a flying Frisbee, soar through the air, and catch the disc in its mouth. It's really fun to watch, but a Frisbee dog isn't born with amazing skill—he (or she) must be trained. Here are the methods I used to teach Whirlin' Wizard, my border collie, who retired undefeated as a Frisbee champion. (Now he's ten and a half years old and taking a well-deserved rest by the fireplace.)

Dogs love to run, jump, chase things, and use their mouths. What activity gives them all this fun with just one throw? Frisbee! It's also fun for you, and it teaches you how to work with an animal and be a responsible pet owner.

Choosing a dog

A dog should fit easily into your living arrangements so that you can take proper care of him and you'll both be happy. For instance, if you live in a small city apartment, don't get a border collie, which is a sheepherding dog and needs lots of exercise. The best Frisbee dogs weigh about thirty-five to fifty pounds as adults (heavier dogs aren't great at jumping) and are happy-go-lucky characters who love to chase balls and sticks. World champions have included mutts, Labrador retrievers, border collies, whippets, Australian shepherds, and other breeds. What counts is taking your dog's natural talents and making them better. If he already turns flips in the air, for example, work with him until he gets *really* great at it.

Peter Bloeme has held the men's world Frisbee title, appeared on TV's *Late Night with David Letterman* and *CBS Sports Spectacular,* and is deputy director of the Come 'N Get It Canine Frisbee Championships. The trainer of Whirlin' Wizard, the youngest dog ever to win the world Frisbee crown, he is the author of *Frisbee Dogs: How to Raise, Train, and Compete* and the producer of *Frisbee Dogs: Training Video.*

By the way, the Humane Society is a wonderful place to adopt a pet. It won't cost a lot of money, and you will save a dog's life.

Puppies

A puppy is ready for general training at three months old, but don't throw him a full-size Frisbee until he has his adult teeth, at about six months, or it might knock out his baby teeth. A flying Frisbee could also scare him, because to a puppy it looks huge. Start him on one of the smaller, three-inch flexible discs made by Nylabone, sold in most pet stores.

To introduce him to a regular-size Frisbee, use it as a food dish. Be sure to pick it up after he eats; you don't want him chewing on it for dessert!

Training

You have to get your dog excited about the Frisbee, so he *wants* it. Whenever you take out the disc, make it a big deal and sound happy: "Yes sir, we're gonna play Frisbee! Let's get that Frisbee!" Make him even more excited by teasing gently with the disc. Hold it at his level, and get him to jump or grab at it. But don't let him take it every time; this "keep-away" game will make him want it more. Then roll or slide the disc a short distance on the ground, and encourage him to chase after it. (Even with puppy teeth, he can still pick things up, especially a soft Nylabone disc.) When he grabs it, praise him for being so smart.

The next step is to push your dog away gently, until you're about four feet apart; get him excited about the Frisbee with a little teasing and keep-away. Then throw him a gentle toss, as if you're lifting the Frisbee into the air toward him. Keep the disc level. Your dog will go for it, and a lot of times will catch it. Either way, encourage him; and when he does catch it, give him lots of petting and praise: "Good boy! That's great!"

Free Stuff

To receive a Frisbee-dog training manual and a schedule of canine competitions around the country, send a self-addressed, business-size envelope to:

PRB & Associates
4060-D Peachtree Road, Suite 326
Atlanta, GA 30319

Once he starts catching the Frisbee directly in front of him, teach your dog to catch a leading toss, while he's running in the direction the disc is moving. With your dog on your left side, hold the disc in front of you and toss it straight up; he'll move across you to catch it. Once he can do that, toss it a few feet away from you. Since your dog knows that the game is to run and catch the Frisbee, he'll quickly learn to go after it. Now work up to longer distances. Within a month or two, he'll be able to catch a ten- or fifteen-yard throw.

Two things to watch out for during training:

1. You don't want your dog to let the Frisbee hit the ground and then grab it. If he does, hold him back with your left hand and pick up the disc with your right. He'll soon get the idea that if he wants the Frisbee, he has to catch it in the air.

2. It's important that your dog bring the Frisbee back to you — but don't be surprised if at first he doesn't. Dogs like to play keep-away. To correct this, put a long cord on your dog and call him to you. If he hesitates, gently pull him back, while you compliment him as if it was his idea in the first place. At this point, don't worry if he doesn't bring you the Frisbee; you just want him to come when you call.

Jumping

The way to get your dog to run, leap, and catch is by holding the Frisbee above his head. Be sure your dog is at least a year old before he starts jumping, so his muscles are properly developed. First, you must teach him the word "take." You can start when he's a puppy and naturally grabs for a Frisbee. It's simple:

As he takes the disc from your hand, say "take." Pretty soon he'll link this word with grabbing the disc.

Use the word "take" to teach your dog to jump. Hold the Frisbee over his head, just a few inches at first, and say "take." He'll leap for the disc.

Once your dog can jump and grab the Frisbee, try a new trick — have him leap over your leg. Start low: Kneel on the ground with your dog on your right side and stick out your left leg. Hold the Frisbee above your leg with your left hand and say "take." At first your dog might run around you and take the Frisbee out of your hand. To prevent this, have a friend stand beside you to block the dog, or practice the trick next to a wall or fence.

Get your dog psyched up first — "Grab the Frisbee; go get it!" — and if your leg is low, he'll jump over it and take the disc. Next time raise your leg a little. Then stand up and put your leg straight out. Eventually, you can flip the Frisbee for him to catch as he jumps over your leg.

Another trick: Hang the Frisbee from your mouth and say "take."

Flips

In this stunt, your dog catches the disc while spinning his body to your left (front flip) or right (back flip). Start by kneeling about four feet away and facing him. You're going to toss the Frisbee vertically (on edge) instead of horizontally (flat). Throw it just over his head, so he has to rise off his front legs to get it. Give him lots of praise and petting! Throw it higher now, so he has to stand up on his back feet. Then toss it even higher and slightly to the side; he'll catch it and sort of fall backwards, landing sideways. Be ready to support him if he's going to come down poorly. The basic is idea is to throw the disc a little higher each time, until he's jumping for it and pretty much spinning sideways on his own.

Tipping

This is an original trick that Wizard and I borrowed from human Frisbee competition, where a person bounces a disc off his fingertip or foot. It's difficult to teach, because your dog has learned to catch the Frisbee and suddenly you're telling him *not* to catch it. Kneel in front of him and hold his collar with

A Few Tips on Training Your Dog

■ Pick a safe area, away from streets. Don't train your dog on asphalt or cement, because the surface will tear up the pads on his feet; if the weather is hot, his feet can get burned. Find a flat, grassy area with no trash, glass, or trees to run into.

■ Remember, a dog doesn't know what you want him to do until you teach him. For example, the first time you say "Shake hands!" your dog will have no idea what you're talking about. So, if he doesn't shake hands, don't yell at him. You have to show him. This is especially true for disc training.

■ The simplest way to train your dog is the most natural way. When he does something all by himself, immediately say the "command" word. If he sits, you say "Sit!" and then "Good boy!" Pretty soon, he'll associate the word with whatever he did. At that point you can use the word as a command: Say "Sit," and he'll sit down.

■ When your dog does the right thing, make a big deal out of it, with lots of praise and petting. But if he fails, never shout at him or say, "Bad boy!" That would give him the message, "If I hang around this kid, he's going to yell and scream at me." (Needless to say, *never* hit your dog.) Keep everything positive, so he feels encouraged and has a good time. That way he'll learn faster.

■ Imagine yourself in your dog's place. Let's say you're teaching him to jump over a box two feet high. He can't see what's on the other side, so when you try to get him to jump, he'll hesitate. (It's as if you led a person to the edge of a cliff and said "Jump!") Help him over the box the first few times, until he knows it's safe. This way you take into account the dog's view of things.

■ Your dog has a short attention span, so work on Frisbee tricks for short periods of time—no more than ten minutes, three times a day.

your left hand, then softly flip the Frisbee just over his head. (Toss it upside down, which will give him a bigger flat area to tip.) Normally, he'd rise up on his hind legs and catch the disc, but by holding his collar you prevent that. He can't change his position, so the Frisbee hits him gently on the nose. Say "tip" at the same time that it bounces off his nose, and then "Good boy! good boy!" After a few tries, your dog will start to understand. With some practice you can let go of him entirely, and he'll hit the disc to you with his nose. He's tipping!

You can extend this trick, so he'll tip the Frisbee and catch it himself. Say "tip" as he bounces the disc off his nose; when you catch it, say "catch" and immediately flip it back to him. Keep cutting down the time between the catch and throw. After a while, don't catch the Frisbee at all. You throw the disc to your dog; he taps it; you say "catch"—but now you move your hand out of the way. Because he's so used to your catching the Frisbee and flipping it to him, he'll just open his mouth and grab the disc.

He's a Frisbee dog!

How to Build Mighty Biceps

by Arnold Schwarzenegger

Arnold Schwarzenegger is chairman of the President's Council on Physical Fitness and Sports, visiting schools all around the country to teach kids about health and exercise. He is the author of the Arnold's Fitness For Kids series, which includes volumes for kids aged six to ten and eleven to fourteen.

I'm not saying you need big muscles like mine to be healthy, but everybody knows that it's better to have strong muscles than weak ones—and that goes for girls as well as boys. I don't believe that boys and girls under sixteen should train with weights, so here's my secret for building strong biceps by lifting...books!

■ Stand holding two books of equal weight, one in each hand (palms up), out in front of you.

■ One arm at a time, raise the book up toward your chin slowly and lower back down slowly, alternating arms.

■ Do this fives times on each arm at first, working up to fifteen times on each arm. To make this harder, you can use heavier books.

Fitness isn't like taking medicine—it's simply living in a way that enables you to develop a body that is strong, flexible, and healthy enough to do all the things in life you want to do with it. That's what I want for *you!*

Take Great Vacation Photographs

by Jodi Cobb

When you get back home from a vacation and look at your photos, what do you see? Your family standing in front of a famous sight like the Grand Canyon? A tourist landmark like the Eiffel Tower in Paris? Or do your pictures really reveal something important about the place, the local people — and maybe about yourself?

I've been able to travel around the world taking pictures for the National Geographic Society. Here are a few things I've learned.

Shoot pictures of what really interests you

You don't have to go along snapping photos of everything you see. Don't take a picture just because the tour guide says that a building is an important architectural monument. Maybe you don't *like* architecture! Maybe you'd rather turn around and look the other way — where you discover that people are having to fill their water buckets from a well and carry them a long, tough way back to their village. A photograph of that scene is just as valid as a shot of the architectural wonder the guide points out.

When you travel, look for things that you love (or hate). Maybe you're intrigued by other kids your age and what they do all day. You notice the ways they're different from you, and also the same. Maybe your interest is fashion, trains, plant life, or hairstyles. By following this interest, you develop a point of

A staff photographer for the National Geographic Society, Jodi Cobb was the first woman to be named White House Photographer of the Year. She has traveled all over the world, including a 7,000-mile trip across China in 1980 as one of the first Westerners to revisit places long closed to outsiders.

view about the places you see and the people you meet. You discover that you feel a certain way about them, and this will be reflected in your photographs. Your point of view remains a constant as you travel from place to place, and you explore it and develop it as you hone your skills.

As an example, I'm interested in women's roles in different cultures of the world. In Saudi Arabia I photographed women whose faces are hidden behind veils. In Japan I became so fascinated by the geisha (women who dance, sing, and converse at men's social gatherings) that I compiled all of my photographs of them into a book.

Compose your pictures well

Decide on your center of interest and fill the frame with it. You don't want people to look like ants in the distance. Move in close to your subject.

Be aware of the background. The classic result of the photographer not being aware of the background is the photo of someone who appears to have a telephone pole growing out of his head. If there are too many obstacles behind your subject, maybe you'll want to move to a different position.

Remember that everything you include in the picture adds to the sum of the photograph. You want the background to be there for a reason. A big mistake made by beginning photographers is to think that only the person's face counts. *All* parts of the rectangle add something to the photograph. Make each part interesting.

These parts of the picture can help to place people in their environments. We've all seen a million photographs of the poor woman in Nepal sitting on a street corner—in fact, it's probably always the same woman—and she's doing nothing but staring at the foreign photographer. Instead, take a little more time and effort to talk to people. Maybe you'll be invited to visit them at home. Then your photographs will tell something about their lives, instead of ending up as boring, static snapshots.

Learn about light

The best light usually comes in the morning and late afternoon. Because the sun is lower on the horizon, the light is soft and warm, and shadows aren't harsh.

Notice where shadows come from. If you take a picture of a person's face at noon, when the sun is overhead, the eyes become black holes and the nose becomes a big white triangle. In that situation you may want to move the person into the shade, where the light is even and balanced. Or use a flash on the person's face, in order to fill in harsh shadows with light. (Don't think a flash is only for indoors!)

Take pictures in all kinds of weather

It doesn't have to be a sunny day. Some of your best pictures can be in bad weather—people running through the rain, umbrellas, water droplets on windowpanes that you can shoot through. Some cultures ignore rain completely and go about their daily business, which can make very interesting photographs. In pictures of monsoon rains in Asia I've seen people sitting in a house with water up to their waists, just as if nothing unusual was going on. In China you see people wearing straw raincoats and bicycling in the rain.

Another idea is to shoot frost patterns on a window. And the dull light of overcast days can be very pretty on film.

Tell a story

Try to create a story in pictures. Think about what you'd *tell* someone about your trip. Then think about how to capture it on film. To make your story more interesting, vary your pictures. Take long shots, medium shots, close-ups, and small details.

Wherever you visit, find out what's going on away from the usual tourist route. Are there any festivals or ceremonies? (In Taiwan you might see people dressed up in costumes and it turns out to be a funeral.) Is there a circus in town? Circuses in other cultures are very different from ours. In China I saw performing pandas!

Approach people as people, not simply as camera subjects

When you go somewhere, think about what it means to the people to *live* there. When you show interest in people and their lives, they're flattered and respond to you. On the other hand, if you race up to them, snap the picture, and walk away, they'll feel that you took advantage of them. The Caribbean islands are ruined for photographers because of this—if you go to a marketplace with a camera, the old ladies sometimes throw lemons and conch shells at you. This is because they have been abused by photographers who don't even talk to them, but just stick a camera in their face.

It's a nice idea to give something back. If you have a Polaroid, hand your subject a picture. If someone asks you to send a print later, and you promise you will, then do it. American kids don't have any idea how much people appreciate it when you send them a photo. All over the world people have shown me letters and pictures of themselves taken with Americans. They are proud possessions.

After all, what you remember most about a trip is the people you meet, not the scenery. And a good way to meet people is with a camera in your hand. By treating others with politeness and respect, you'll make friends, and friendships can change your life. And your pictures will say more because you'll understand something about the people you're photographing.

See for yourself

Your photographs don't have to look like pictures you've seen before. You don't have to follow anyone else's rules. When you look over your pictures, you may discover something very important—who *you* are and what you're really interested in. Photography is a way to learn about the world, but it's also a way to learn about yourself.

How to Cartoon

by Sergio Aragonés

Sergio Aragonés has been a cartoonist for *MAD* since 1962. He created the magazine's Marginals — uncaptioned gags that appear in the white space around the edges of the page. He also draws his own comic book about a wandering barbarian named Groo, which is printed in ten languages.

Cartooning is a great way to make a living. You do what you did in the third grade — and they pay you for it! "Serious" artists hate to have people laugh at their drawings, but to a cartoonist, laughter is a sweet sound. Here are some tips on how to draw cartoons.

Exaggeration is the key to cartooning. You take real life and overstate it, especially in drawing facial expressions. When your character laughs, snarls, or makes any other expression, use all the face he's got. For some reason, it's also funny to give him a big nose and set his eyes a bit too close together.

When drawing **action**, again, there is no limit to the exaggeration you can use. In this example, the first drawing depicts a man running in real life; the second shows how he looks in a cartoon. It's the same for the poor guy who just hit his thumb with a hammer. Exaggeration means drawing things wilder and funnier than they are in real life.

When you draw **animals**, exaggerate their special features for a comic effect. Each drawing can tell a short, funny story. (In fact, I consider myself a writer as much as an artist.)

Use yourself as a model and **pose** in the mirror. Exaggerate the movements. Also pay attention to **clothing** and other things that help identify your character—a Dracula cape or a karate belt, a baseball bat or a diamond miner's pick.

TRICKS OF THE TRADE FOR KIDS

Learning how to draw exaggerated movements and funny noses, however, is the easiest part of being a cartoonist. Learning how to think of **funny ideas** may be a bit harder.

Use an everyday object in an unexpected way. This changes the usual view of something into a comically unusual one.

Visualize a common scene with an offbeat complication.

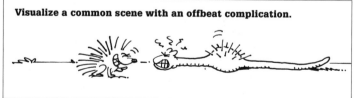

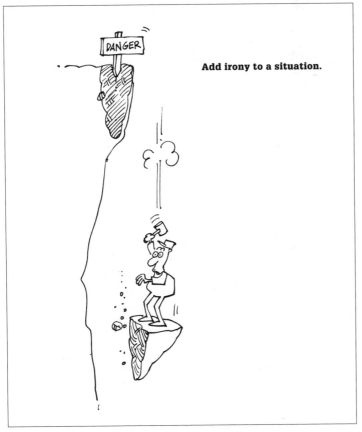

Add irony to a situation.

Staying loose in your drawing style will help you stay loose in your gags as well. It's like being a circus clown, which is much easier and more fun in a silly clown suit. That's what your drawing style is—your clown suit.

Tail a Criminal like the FBI Does
by Regis Boyle

Now retired from the FBI, Regis Boyle received commendation citations from J. Edgar Hoover and every FBI director since. Although an expert marksman, he always preferred to talk his way out of a bad situation. During his career, he protected the Attorney General of the United States and captured scores of dangerous criminals.

During my twenty-year career with the FBI, I investigated what they call the "heavies"—crimes such as kidnappings and airplane hijackings. I had to follow bad guys around cities and sometimes all over the country. Following someone surreptitiously is called surveillance—a TV detective might call it tailing or shadowing—and it involves some clever tricks. To follow a criminal at night in his car, you might break one of his taillights, making it easy to spot him (the crook has a white taillight and all the other cars have red ones).

Surveillance sometimes goes on for a long time. Once I captured a fugitive (a criminal running from justice) who was on the FBI's Ten Most Wanted list—but I had to track him down for six months. Tailing someone is not an easy job. There's an art to it, and it takes a lot of practice. Luckily, it's something you can practice on anyone—even your friends, your parents, or the mailman. Here are some suggestions.

1. Try to blend in with the crowd. If everyone on the street is wearing coats and ties, but you're wearing a clown suit, you'll be obvious because you stand out. On the other hand, if you're tailing a guy who works at the circus, wearing a clown suit may be a great idea.

2. Keep your subject (the person you are following) in sight at all times. If you lose him even for a second, you may have lost him forever.

3. Change sides of the street once in a while. If you cross the street, he's less likely to spot you than if you walk right behind him.

4. Never stop directly across the street from him. When he looks in a store window, your reflection will appear.

5. Change your clothes as you go. It's odd, but taking something *off* can be just as good a disguise as putting something on. Let's say you've been wearing a baseball cap but then remove it; you look like a different person. Changing clothes also helps you blend in: If a guy I was following went to a baseball game, I'd take off my shirt and necktie and attend the game in my T-shirt. Now I'm just part of the crowd.

6. Don't stop exactly when he does. In old movies, when a bad guy stops on the sidewalk, the detective also pauses, pulls out a newspaper, and stands on the street corner pretending to read it. In real life, you don't want to be seen waiting on the street; it's too obvious. Instead, step into a doorway or between some buildings. An even better idea is to walk past the subject, go into a store, and watch him through the window. He can't see you because of the reflections in the glass!

7. Never look the person in the eye. It's a giveaway. The subject glances around and catches *you* looking at *him*. He wonders, "Who *is* this guy?" and that starts him thinking. There's something about eye contact: Looking a person in the eye creates a direct connection between the two of you, establishes a relationship, even if the other person is unsure of what it is.

8. Never admit that you're tailing him. If the subject turns and accuses you of following him, just walk away. Or say: "Are you nuts? I didn't even know you were there!" Criminals often are so nervous and suspicious that they think *everyone* is following them. If you deny it, they'll probably walk away and never think anything of it. And then you just continue to follow them…

Once I tailed a bookie (someone who takes illegal bets on sports) into a tobacco shop in Portland, Oregon. We struck up a conversation, and he started telling me that he was being followed by the FBI. The shop owner said, "You're crazy; you think the FBI's following you all the time." The bookie said, "It's true! Look around out there!" So I went to the window and told him, "I don't see anybody." He said, "Yeah, they're out there!" I went outside again and continued to follow him.

9. Change strategies, depending on where he goes. If the subject goes into a store, watch him through the window. (He can't see you, but you can see him.) If he goes into an office building, though, go in with him. Get on the elevator with him, and push the button for the floor above the one he does. If a crowd of people gets off at his floor, you get off too. (You'll blend in.) If he gets off alone, go one floor higher and walk down the stairs one flight. Look for him; maybe you can find out who he's meeting. If you can't spot him quickly, go back downstairs and wait for him outside the building.

10. You don't have to travel on foot. Bicycles, roller skates, and skateboards all can be used to great advantage. In heavy traffic, for example, bikes can move faster than cars. In the FBI we've also used airplanes, motorcycles, helicopters, trucks—you name it. Such vehicles are good disguises—would you think that a truck driver was actually an FBI agent?

11. Don't try to guess where the subject is going next. He may not show up. He may have changed his plans. He may have forgotten something and gone back home.

12. If you lose the subject, go back to the last place you saw him. Your odds are better than if you just started wandering around, hoping to spot him. He may have stepped into a store or office building and will be back out in a minute.

You may wonder what takes place if someone realizes that he's being followed. It happens sometimes. A suspected bank robber in Oregon actually started waving at me. He'd come out of a building and yelled where he was going next, to save me some trouble. He's been in jail since 1973. That'll teach him to wave at an FBI man!

Do Hand Tricks Just like "Thing" in the Addams Family Movies

by Christopher Hart

Christopher Hart plays the part of "Thing" in the Addams Family movies. A professional magician, he was honored as Stage Magician of the Year by Hollywood's conjurors club, the Magic Castle. He performs in Las Vegas, Atlantic City, Japan, and Europe.

In the Addams Family movies, my hand plays the part of "Thing"—you know, the hand that walks around by itself, with no body attached. (To learn the secret of this illusion, see "How Special Effects Helped Create 'Thing.'") My part is to make Thing seem human.

When I first tried out for the role, the director said, "Okay, how would your hand look happy?" So I made my hand jump up and down like an excited little puppy dog. "How about nervous?" he said. For that emotion I kept my fingertips on the table, relaxed my hand, and just quivered it back and forth. (Try it! It really looks like someone trembling.)

Here's how to create a little stage play starring your own hand. To make it interesting, let's turn your hand into a puppet—an octopus. First, take an old black sock and cut off the tip. Slip it over your arm, covering the area from your wrist to your elbow. Now paint your hand a light or bright color (with washable, nontoxic paint!) from your fingertips to your wrist. Use whatever color

you want your octopus to be. On the back of your hand, paint some big, funny-looking eyes. Because your arm is in a black sleeve, it seems to fade away. The audience just sees the "octopus."

You can build a puppet theater to make this tricky illusion look even better. Take a cardboard grocery box and cut out a rectangular hole in the front. That will be the stage opening. Paint the inside of the box with flat (not glossy) black paint. You only need to paint the back and sides. Cut out a strip about four

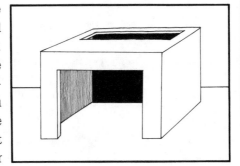

inches wide from the top of the box, along the rear, where you can insert your arm. With your arm inside the box, the black sock blends into the black background. From the front, all that shows is your brightly painted hand. No one can see that it's connected to your arm!

If you want to get fancy, you can "dress the set" (as moviemakers say) to look like an underwater scene in the ocean. On the bottom of the box paste some rocks, paper starfish, and a small pirate's chest. If you want to add some seaweed, string a few strips of green crepe paper on thread or some fishing line, and hang them from the top of the box. The "seaweed" also masks your arm, adding to the illusion that your octopus-hand is running around by itself on the ocean floor.

All you need to do now is invite an audience to your show. (To learn how to make your hand act out different feelings and situations, see "Okay, Thing—Look Happy!")

I'm just glad I could "give you a hand"!

The Living Hand in the Paper Bag

Here's another great hand trick. Imagine you have a paper bag resting on the palm of your right hand. Your left hand is holding the top edge. And then a *third* hand pops out the top of the sack! It's like having a "Thing Bag." And this little trick is easy to do.

Take a paper grocery bag, and cut out a hole in the back. (You're going to stick your real right arm through this hole when you do the trick.) Stuff a glove with something like Kleenex, and tape it to the bottom front of the bag. It should be palm up-

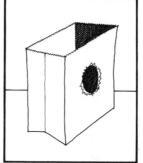

ward, with the fingers toward the front. It looks as though the bag is resting on this "hand." Put the other glove on your left hand, and use that hand to steady the top edge of the bag. Insert your real right arm through the hole in the back of the bag.

Now go up to someone, ask if they'd like to see something weird—and make your hand pop out of the sack! Aaagghhhh!

Okay, Thing—Look Happy! Turning Your Hand into a Hollywood Actor

In the Addams Family movies, Thing has acted out all kinds of parts, from being frightened to falling asleep. Here are a few ideas you can use to make Thing seem human.

Frightened Thing: To make Thing look scared, hold your hand palm down, with fingertips touching the ground. You're going to bend your wrist back, so your fingers come off the ground and your palm faces toward whatever Thing is scared of. As you do, curl your fingers like a claw, instead of keeping them flat. Do the whole thing quickly. It will look as if Thing rears up in fear, then goes back down.

I used this in a scene with Christopher Lloyd, who plays Fester. Thing was driving a car, with Fester on the seat next to him. We were swerving through oncoming traffic. As the camera rolled, I tugged the wheel left and right. Then the director would say, "Okay, here comes a car right at you!" Thing would jump up into his scared pose, and go back down. It was very comical.

Happy Thing: Let's say you want your hand to jump up like an excited puppy. Hold your hand palm down, with your fingertips touching the floor. Flex your hand downward, bending all your finger joints. (It's almost like you're bending your legs at the knees, but using your hand instead.) Now your hand springs up like a pogo stick. As you jump in the air, wiggle your fingers. It looks like your hand is saying "Wheeeee!"

Sleeping Thing: Once Morticia was painting a picture of Thing, who falls asleep as he's posing. To do that, I relaxed my fingers and then slowly lifted the back of my hand up and down. It looked as if Thing was breathing deeply, the way you do when you're asleep. (Of course, the moviemakers added sound effects to heighten the illusion.)

Thing skidding to a stop: Imagine you want Thing to race along the floor and then put on the brakes. Make your hand skitter along as fast as you can. Then spread out all your fingers and keep your hand moving forward. It looks as if Thing is sliding to a halt.

How Special Effects Helped Create "Thing" for the Addams Family Movies

How can Thing appear to be just a hand, with no body? Special effects! Let's imagine that Thing is supposed to run down a hallway. I wear a black sleeve on my arm and a rubber wrist piece, which looks like the top of Thing. I lie facedown on a cart with my arm stretched out to the side, and someone pushes the cart. I make Thing run by skittering my fingers along the floor.

On film you can see the cart and my arm (even though my arm is in a black sleeve). After that first shot, they film the whole scene a second time without me. The camera is run by a computer that can duplicate the same movement again and again. They put the camera back where it started and it follows the same path it did the first time. But now I'm not in the picture. The camera shoots a background scene that exactly matches what I just did.

In the special-effects lab, technicians erase all of me but my hand from the first piece of film, working frame by frame. That leaves a transparent "hole" in the picture where I used to be. They lay that hole over the second piece of film, which fills in the background.

In the finished movie, all you see is an unattached hand running down the hallway. It's like magic.

Five Tips on Being a Great Cheerleader

by Stephanie Breaux

What makes cheerleaders great? They have a special ability to fire people up for their team. Since cheerleading has become an athletic event, they practice with dedication and keep themselves in top physical condition. And because cheerleaders are so visible in school, they realize their responsibility as leaders. Whether you're a girl or a boy — there are lots of coed squads now — here are some tips on how to be a great cheerleader.

Stephanie Breaux was a cheerleader at Louisiana State University and now cheers on the coed squad of the Kansas City Chiefs. She works with the International Cheerleading Foundation in Shawnee Mission, Kansas, where she oversees cheerleading instruction for camps around the nation and in several foreign countries.

Project energy into the crowd

Crowds are sometimes shy about yelling; they think that cheering is the cheerleaders' job. So you need to get them involved. The secret is using short words that people won't be scared to yell along with you and that are easy to remember — like "Go!" and "Defense!" Another trick is holding up a sign that says "GO" or "FIGHT" in big letters. This draws the crowd's attention to the sidelines and gets them involved in cheering.

Stunts also get crowds excited. Probably the most popular, because it's so much fun to watch, is the basket toss. Three cheerleaders toss a fourth one straight up in the air and then catch her. (College squads that include boys can get their girls thirty feet in the air!) The basket toss is a big crowd pleaser, but safety has to be your top priority. A coach should teach you the proper technique, and you must always use spotters (experienced people that catch anyone who falls) when doing any stunt.

One of the latest ways to get crowds excited is by using music and dancing. If the cheerleaders dance to a high-energy song with a great beat, something that's total funk, the energy is contagious—just like at a rock concert.

Make direct eye contact with the crowd

If you look people straight in the face, saying "Yell with us!" they'll be more willing to do it. But if you look down at the ground, you could scream your lungs out and not get a response. Let your crowd know that you want them to cheer with you! It's also the cheerleaders' responsibility to be sure that fans show good sportsmanship during the game, and the squad should set an example by their great attitude.

When you jump, keep your head and shoulders up

As soon as your head goes down, your body goes down, too. So if you want to make higher jumps, look up! Your shoulders and head will guide your body. A tip: Be sure to stretch every day, so you have good flexibility for jumping.

Be sharp

The more quickly you do a motion, such as raising and lowering pompons, the sharper and cleaner it looks. If you move too slowly, the group looks sloppy. It also looks better if you make your motions nice and big.

Never scream

Strangely enough, cheerleaders should never scream. If you come out and scream "Woooo!!!" you'll really strain your voice. What you should do is to yell distinct, short words, like "Go! Fight! Win!" If the whole squad yells the same word, it will be louder and no one person will have to yell her head off. Also hold up signs, which can be seen by people sitting at the top of the stands, even if they can't hear you above the crowd noise.

Cheerleaders can also join "band chants." A school band often comes up with drum cadences that are short and fun, and the cheerleaders can get in on the action by incorporating a yell into it. The crowd likes being part of the band and the beat, so they roar along with the music.

If you decide you want to be cheerleader, an easy way to break in is to watch older cheerleaders. Learn from them and follow their footsteps. The most important point is to have a positive attitude. And don't forget to smile!

How to Be a Genius

by Thomas Armstrong

Educational con-
sultant, writer, and
former teacher
Thomas Armstrong
is the author of
***Awakening Your
Child's Natural
Genius*** and ***Seven
Kinds of Smart.***

The way to be a genius is to realize that you *already* are a genius. If you don't feel like one, it's probably because your genius is sleeping inside of you and just needs to be awakened.

Of course, if we define "genius" in a narrow way, then a lot of people get left out. But a genius isn't only a person who carries a pocket calculator and solves test problems fast. In fact, plenty of geniuses didn't do well on tests—including Einstein, who felt that his best ideas came from his own imagination. Studies show that there are at least seven different ways of being "smart." We might label these as word-smart, number-smart, picture-smart (being artistic), music-smart, body-smart (being athletic or good at making things), people-smart (understanding others), and self-smart (understanding your personality and talents).

You may be a genius at any of these. But if this genius is slumbering, how can you tickle it awake? Here are some ideas.

1. Pay attention to what *really* interests you in life. It may not be something that other people consider to be genius-like behavior. But remember that there are geniuses on the hockey rink, in the auto repair garage, in the art studio—in every walk of life. The point is to discover *your* genius, and the best way to do this is to explore what really fascinates you. It may be a hobby such as stamp collecting or putting together models; it may be drawing or singing. Once you find it, fan the flames of that interest.

2. Find an adult who can help draw out your genius — someone who not only sees your talents, but also pushes you along when you get discouraged or bored and feel like giving up. (There are always slumps as a person develops his or her genius.) The adult may be a parent, a relative, a teacher, or someone in your community.

If you're at least of junior high school age, you might look for a person in your area to whom you could apprentice yourself. (An apprentice is a beginner who finds a master to learn from.) If you like writing, you could ask the editor of your local newspaper to let you come to the office and learn the trade of journalism. If you love jewelry, seek out a jeweler who's willing to show you how to work with silver and stones. (In return, you could help out with chores.)

3. Think about what resources you'll need to develop your genius. For a stamp collector, these resources could include a stamp club where you'll learn about and trade stamps; you also may need to earn money to buy stamps. However, if your talent is running, all you need is a good pair of sneakers; the rest is blood, sweat, and tears out on the track.

4. Even though you're talented, you still have to work hard to be great. The famous inventor Thomas Edison said, "Genius is one percent inspiration and ninety-nine percent perspiration." You are born with some of your genius, but the rest you have to develop.

5. Regularly set aside time to foster your genius. You probably do this already if you play a sport, practice music, or spend a lot of time reading. But if not, consider spending even fifteen minutes a day to work at what you do best. Don't get so saddled with homework and chores that you fail to nourish your talent.

6. Keep your mind active and open to new ideas. What are you reading now? What are you interested in? Sometimes television can introduce new worlds to you. You can learn how people live in a Brazilian rainforest or watch government leaders make decisions. But you must make good choices. Don't watch mind-numbing programs or spend all your time playing Nintendo — unless you think that your genius is to write TV shows or to develop computer software.

7. Explore the world and expose yourself to a wide range of things. Don't spend *all* your time cultivating your main talent — you may have hidden talents that you don't know about yet that must be awakened through other means. Even if you're not athletic, go out and try sports once in a while. Read a book about something you never even knew existed. The goal is to stay focused on whatever you love most and do best, but at the same time to live a balanced life.

You might think of your genius as a genie, like the one in the story about Aladdin and the magic lamp. The lamp holds the genie's great power and creativity, a kind of magic that can take many different shapes. The genie is what lies inside all of us. You just have to rub your own lamp to find it.

How to Be a Success

by Mister Rogers, Judy Blume, Lee Iacocca, and Richard Dean "MacGyver" Anderson, as told to the Roosevelt Middle School of Decatur, Illinois

You've already learned much about what it takes to be successful in school. It's much the same no matter what school you're attending or what work you're doing. To me, what makes someone successful is managing a healthy combination of wishing and doing. Wishing doesn't make anything happen, but it certainly can be the start of some important happenings. I hope you'll feel good enough about yourself, your yesterdays, and your todays, that you'll wish and dream all you can. And that you'll do all you can to help the best of your wishes come true. **— Fred Rogers**

The most important part of education is learning you can *think* for yourself. And thinking for yourself will be the single most important part of the rest of your life. That means seeing your options, weighing the pros and cons, learning to make wise decisions, taking responsibility for your own actions. It also means being aware of other people's feelings. Okay, so you'll make some mistakes along the way. We all do. But at least they'll be *your* mistakes. And you'll learn from them, too.
—Judy Blume

Fred Rogers is the host of "Mister Rogers' Neighborhood," the longest-running children's program on TV, reaching 7 million families a week.

Judy Blume is one of America's most read, most loved writers for young people. In her books she uses humor and honesty in bringing to light feelings her readers recognize as their own.

Lee Iacocca is the former chairman of the board of the Chrysler Corporation, one of America's largest automobile makers.

I have found that in order to become successful, you must determine what you want, and then be willing to work tirelessly to reach your goal. The people I know who have become successful have done just that.

The best advice I can give you is to get a good education; it'll help prepare you for whatever career you choose.

—Lee Iacocca

Richard Dean Anderson starred in the TV series "MacGyver," portraying a hero who relied on knowledge and quick thinking, not fists and guns, to defeat the bad guys.

Think first. Think fast. Be careful. Pursue. Be great!!

—Richard Dean Anderson

As a class project, the eighth grade at the Roosevelt Middle School in Decatur, Illinois, asked successful people for good advice to students entering high school. The responses included these words of guidance.

Tie a Knot That Will Never Come Undone (Until You Want It To)

by Dennis Conner

The most useful knot you can tie is called a bowline. It not only attaches things securely, but is easy to untie. It doesn't tighten up on itself the way a knot in your shoelaces does. Instead, a bowline forms a loop of rope that won't slip or change its size. A bowline has all sorts of uses. For instance, with this handy knot a sailor can take a rope that is secured to the boat and tie it to a metal ring on the dock.

Dennis Conner has skippered the winning yacht four times in the America's Cup, the world championship of sailing. A resident of California, he joined the San Diego Yacht Club at age eleven and has won races in boats from 11 feet to 80 feet long.

In everyday life you can use a bowline to fasten almost anything to something else. Here's how to tie a bowline in four easy steps.

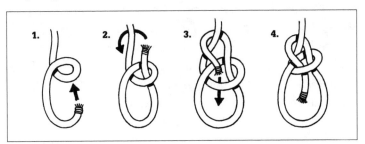

An easy trick for recalling the steps is to say to yourself, "A rabbit pops out of his hole, goes around the tree, and then goes down into his hole again." This is the way everybody remembers how to tie a bowline—even the most seasoned sailors in the world.

To untie a bowline, just grasp the "tree" part of the line and push it down into the "hole" part of the knot. The knot will loosen, making it easy to untie.

Make a Wacky Video with Trick Photography

by Bob Wise

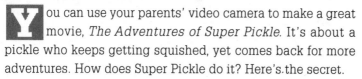

You can use your parents' video camera to make a great movie, *The Adventures of Super Pickle*. It's about a pickle who keeps getting squished, yet comes back for more adventures. How does Super Pickle do it? Here's.the secret.

First, you need three or four "doubles" for Super Pickle. That's because each time Super Pickle gets mashed, a new pickle that looks identical takes his place for the next adventure. To get enough doubles, you'll need to search through a few jars of pickles. The doubles have to look almost exactly alike, so the audience will accept them as being the same pickle during the whole movie. All doubles should be the same size and color, have similar bumps, and so on.

When Super Pickle appears in a scene with other pickles, the audience needs to know which one he is. It might be a good idea to make a cape for him to wear.

Now let's set up some adventures for Super Pickle. Say you've got him and a pickle pal standing on the edge of a balcony. Start the camera, focus on the pickles, and talk in a high pickle voice. (Super Pickle doesn't actually move, but his voice makes him seem alive. If you want, a friend can play the part of one pickle, as long as he or she doesn't get in front of the camera.) The two pickles are chatting: "The view from way up here is so beautiful, don't you think?" "I used to get dizzy when I looked down," says Super Pickle. "Whoa!"

Bob Wise is a director for the hit TV series "Unsolved Mysteries." He began as a cameraman on the show in 1986.

Now turn off the camera and move to a different angle, somewhere below the balcony. Start the camera again as Super Pickle falls off the balcony! (Someone off-camera can push him, or you can attach a transparent fishing line and tug him over.)

As Super Pickle falls, he screams "AAAgghhhh!" Meanwhile, "pan" the camera (follow the pickle as it falls). Just before Super Pickle hits the ground, turn off the camera.

Here's the tricky part. Place a pickle on the ground and "presquish" it with your shoe. (The flatter it is, the funnier.) Step back and start the camera again. Make a fast movement downward with the camera to reveal the squashed pickle on the ground. At the same time, make a noise like a pickle hitting the ground and going splat.

By moving the camera at the beginning of this last shot, you can hide the "cut" and trick the audience into thinking they really saw the pickle fall all the way to the ground. To finish the scene, poor Super Pickle's muffled little voice might say, "Don't worry; I'm fine, I'm fine!"

Because you have plenty of "doubles" waiting in the wings, Super Pickle can go on to his next adventure. It will end, of course, with getting squished again. For this one, ask your dad or mom to help. During the scene they'll drive the car a few feet in your driveway. The action starts with our hero and another pickle standing on the curb. The other pickle says, "You better not go! You better not go!" Super Pickle says, "No problem. I have the right of way!" You cut to Super Pickle standing out in the middle of the driveway. Then cut back to the pickle that

The Mystery of the Disappearing Alien

Here's how to make a short movie with trick photography. A person is chatting with an alien from outer space. Suddenly the alien looks at his watch and says, "Uh-oh, gotta go!" And he disappears!

The secret: Put your video camera on a tripod and lock it down so nothing can move. Be careful to press the "play" button gently, so you don't jiggle the camera. You'll need two actors; maybe your little brother can dress up as an alien and another person can play the other part. As the scene opens, they're sitting in two chairs, talking. Then the alien looks at his watch and says, "Uh-oh, gotta go!"

Turn off the camera. The person playing the alien runs out of the picture. The other person sits *perfectly still*. Then you start the camera again. If the other person has held his or her position reasonably well, it will look as if the alien vanished!

The person left behind must look astonished. He spins his head, trying to see where the alien might have gone. He says, "Wha—? What happened? Where'd he go? That's pretty weird!" But the mystery is never solved!

A few hints: This video trick depends on having *nothing* change except for the alien disappearing. The other person has to hold absolutely still for the few seconds while the camera is off. And don't try this trick on a windy day, because trees in the background will be moving. When you stop and start the camera, they'll seem to jump in an unnatural way. The best background is something that doesn't move at all, like a building.

Show the videotape to your family and friends. They'll love the "unsolved mystery" of the disappearing alien!

stayed on the curb, zooming in quickly (with the camera's zoom lens) as he cries out, "Oh, noooooo!" (For each cut you turn off the camera, aim it in the new direction, and start the camera again.) When you cut back to Super Pickle this time, he's already underneath the car tire. (You stuck him there when the camera was turned off between shots.) Your dad slowly drives over Super Pickle. After the tire rolls away, we see the flattened remains. Then a little voice says, "Don't worry; I'm fine, I'm fine!"

The next scene might start with two pickles sitting on the kitchen counter. Super Pickle says, "It's great to be back in the safety of our own home, where I can sit back and..." Then your mother's hand comes into the shot, picks up Super Pickle, and cuts him up into slices. The scene ends with the running gag "Don't worry; I'm fine, I'm fine!"

The Adventures of Super Pickle keeps on going until you run out of ideas or videotape—or pickles!

How to Get the Most out of a Book

by LeVar Burton

For entertainment value alone, reading is a remarkable and amazing exercise. You can pick up a book and, in your imagination, travel anywhere in the universe. Not even Nintendo can compete with that!

That is why I think it's so important that we change our beliefs about reading. In this culture, reading is too often thought to be hard, boring, and something that only girls and nerds do. That idea is completely wrong.

There are no limits to what we can be inspired to do, to feel, or to accomplish from reading a book. Every single book I've ever read (and I read about fifty books a year) has enriched my life. I'm not saying that I enjoyed them all. Sometimes I just didn't relate to the subject or didn't find that the author's voice fit very well with my own point of view. Still, every book I've read has made me richer in some way. Without exception! I can't think of very many things in my life that I can say that about.

Here are a few tips on reading:

■ Pick a subject that really interests you; then it's only natural for you to *enjoy* reading.

■ Stay open. What is it that this book causes to stir inside of you? The potential of reading is as limitless as you are.

■ When you read a nonfiction (factual) book, a newspaper, or a magazine article, read with a critical eye—or, let's say, a critical heart. This means taking the information and saying to

LeVar Burton is the host and producer of Reading Rainbow, public television's Emmy Award–winning show devoted to discovering books. He also stars as Lt. Commander Geordi LaForge in Star Trek: The Next Generation, and he played Kunta Kinte in Roots.

yourself, "Does this make sense to me? How does this fit in with everything else I know about the world?" And remember, just because something is in print doesn't necessarily mean it's true!

■ When you read fiction (imaginary stories) for enjoyment, on the other hand, give yourself over to the world of the book. Give your critical mind a rest and allow yourself to be swept up in the story. That's when you begin to discover the joy and enchantment of books. Reading is like a magic carpet, and it can take you anywhere in life you want to go.

How to Steal a Base/ Pick Off a Base Stealer

by Chad Curtis and Mark Langston

Stealing a base

■ **Do** run in the right situation. You've got to know how quick a pitcher is to the plate, and whether a catcher has a good reputation for being able to throw the ball down to second base quickly. Watch and see if they're giving you something that makes it easier for you to steal.

■ **Do** get a good jump. As soon as the pitcher starts his delivery to home, you've got to get a good break to second base. (During practice, work on your speed and your jumps. See how efficient you can be from a starting position to full speed.)

■ **Do** look toward home when you are about halfway to second base. Just glance toward the plate and see what action is taking place there. Did the guy hit the ball? Is the ball in the dirt? Or did the catcher catch it and is ready to throw to second base? After this glance you know what you're supposed to do.

■ **Don't** forget to read the fielder. It's the last thing to do as you slide into second. You need to know which side of the base the fielder is on, so you know where to slide.

■ **Don't** go if you don't get a good jump. One thing a good base stealer will always be able to recognize is when he *doesn't* get a good jump; then he just stops and stays at first. If you're a base stealer, you're aggressive and are going to get picked off from time to time. But you have to minimize those situations so as not to hurt your team.

Chad Curtis, who made the big leagues after being a 45th-round draft selection, stole 43 bases as a rookie for the California Angels.

California Angel Mark Langston led the American League in pick-offs in 1992 and is a four-time winner of the Rawlings Gold Glove Award, given for excellence in fielding.

The pick-off move

Base runners try to steal bases, and pitchers try to pick them off. It's a cat-and-mouse game that's as old as baseball. Here are my tips for you pitchers.

■ **Do** keep the runner close to the base. This gives your catcher a chance to throw him out at second base if he decides to run.

■ **Do** use some strategy. You can throw over to first base easy a couple of times, not very hard. Then, if you feel the runner has a big enough lead, you can make a real quick throw.

■ **Do** fake out the runner. The idea is to mess him up. He thinks you're throwing a pitch to home plate, but you end up throwing to first base. A good way to practice is to stand in front of a mirror and watch yourself making the pick-off move over to first. Be as natural as you can, and make it look as if you're really throwing to home plate.

■ **Don't** throw the ball over to first base just to throw it. A lot of times a pitcher with a four- or five-run lead will do this, but he knows the runners are not going to run in that situation. There's no need to throw the ball over to first base.

■ **Don't** throw the ball away. You want to be aggressive, but you also want to make a good throw. Make sure you throw directly to the first baseman and not into the runner or where the first baseman might not get to it.

■ **Don't** forget about the hitter. Sometimes you can get too caught up in trying to pick somebody off, and you forget about the batter. Then, when you make the pitch, it isn't what you wanted and you're liable to give up a big hit.

How to Read Minds

by Larry Becker

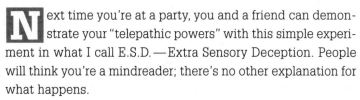ext time you're at a party, you and a friend can demonstrate your "telepathic powers" with this simple experiment in what I call E.S.D. — Extra Sensory Deception. People will think you're a mindreader; there's no other explanation for what happens.

Your friend leaves the room, escorted by someone in your audience. During her absence, you ask a volunteer to whisper any two- or three-digit number in your ear, like 35 or 179. Or he can describe a simple geometric design, like a triangle or circle, or mention a three- or four-letter word. As soon as the volunteer whispers his thought, you write it on a regular three- by five-inch index card and immediately hand it to him for safekeeping. Your friend is called back to the room. Without saying a word, you simply hand her a second index card and a pen. Then you leave the room. Your friend proceeds to receive the volunteer's thoughts, which she notes on the card. Sure enough, when the two cards are compared, they match!

This baffling demonstration requires no secret signals, no codes, no memorizing. All you have to do is place a small piece of Scotch Magic Tape on your left thumbnail (assuming you're right-handed) before performing. It should be just large enough to cover the nail. The only other props you need are two index cards and a black felt-tip pen. Put the cards in your left pocket. After the volunteer has whispered, say, a three-digit number in your ear, take out the pen and one of the index cards, holding

Larry Becker has performed as a psychic entertainer for more than thirty years, lectured for magicians around the world, and created many ESP tricks (including the one he teaches here). He received the Psychic Entertainers Association Achievement Award for outstanding contributions to the art of mentalism.

the card so the volunteer can't see what is being written. Proceed to write his number, first on the tape covering your left thumbnail, and then again on the card itself. When you hold the card in your left hand, your thumb naturally rests near the center of the card, so it's a simple matter to write on the thumbnail. And since the volunteer can't see what you're writing, the double writing of his number will not be seen or suspected. Now take the card in your right hand and give it to the volunteer, asking him to place it out of sight in his pocket. Then ask someone to call your friend back into the room. As she enters, reach into your left pocket and bring out the second index card. Hand her the card and pen with your left hand, thumb on top. A glance at your thumbnail gives her all the information she needs, in a split second, as you pass. Quickly leave the room, at which time you remove the evidence from your thumbnail. The rest is up to her. With intense concentration, she duplicates the volunteer's thought on the card you gave her. When it is compared with the card in the volunteer's possession, it matches! Unfortunately, your friend will get all the applause — but that's showbiz.

When you present mental magic — tricks that look like mindreading — do it in a fun, lighthearted way. Don't take yourself too seriously, acting like a "mysto mindreader." Your goal isn't to appear superior to others, but to entertain them. This trick is so mind-boggling that people may think you've *really* got psychic powers!

Perform Anytime, Anywhere— and Knock 'em Dead

by Happy Traum

Whether you're learning to play a musical instrument, juggle, sing, or perform magic, sooner or later you'll want to try out your new skills on an audience. It may be in a living room for family and friends, at a school assembly, or at a talent show. No matter how large or small the audience, as soon as you come before them, with your magic wand in your hand or a song on your lips, you are *performing*. There are some basic things you should know to help you do your best and give the most pleasure to your audience. (For the sake of discussion, let's assume you're going to play the guitar and sing. But the same tips will help you with any performance.)

An important figure on the American folk music scene for thirty-five years, Happy Traum plays guitar, banjo, and bass, and he has recorded and sung with Bob Dylan. He is the founder of Homespun Tapes in Woodstock, New York, a mail-order company offering music instruction on audio and video tapes by top performing musicians.

Be prepared

Before starting, be sure that your equipment is in good working order and that you have everything you'll need—new strings on your guitar, picks, amplifier, electric cables, and so on. Tune up carefully before going on-stage. Choose songs you know well, and make a list so you know exactly what you'll be playing. You can adapt these rules to any performance, such as a magic show. Have all your props ready and arranged, so you can pick them up without fumbling. Arrange the tricks into a routine, so you don't have to worry about what comes next when you're on-stage.

Relax

Every performer gets the jitters, and a bit of nervous excitement can add spark and intensity to your music. But you don't want to be so frightened that it hampers your playing or tightens up your voice. Take a few quiet moments alone before going on, and consciously try to relax. (You can think happy thoughts, imagine yourself doing a great performance, or just sit calmly.) If you get stage fright, remind yourself that the audience is not there to judge you. People come to a performance expecting that they'll have a good time and be entertained. They will be on your side from the start.

Start with something easy

Your opening song should be one that's easy for you, that you know you can play flawlessly. This will give you confidence, as well as time to adjust to the stage, the lights, and the microphone. You'll be at ease for the rest of your set. Resist the impulse to start by playing your hottest licks to impress the audience. You could find yourself on a tightrope from which you might fall.

In any performance, you must grab the audience's attention immediately. Begin with a tune that is engaging—one that's interesting, up-tempo, or popular. It's much harder to win an audience back after they've lost interest. (That's why it's risky to begin your performance with a long, slow ballad.) Start with a bang.

Build your performance

Arrange your set of songs (or juggling stunts, etc.) to have the greatest impact. After starting strong, you want the performance to flow smoothly and have variety. Like any good dramatic performance, it must have peaks and valleys. (Quieter moments will allow your audience to rest a bit after the high points.) Avoid doing a string of several songs at the same tempo, and if it's a long set, put in some surprises, such as a funny song or an ear-catching instrumental, to change the pace and maintain the audience's interest. Your performance must build to a climax, so save your strongest, most audience-pleasing song for last. And remember the oldest rule of theater: Leave them wanting more. It's better to do one song too few than to overstay your welcome and find your listeners growing restless. If they want more, you can always do an encore!

Develop an air of confidence

The more comfortable you are, the more comfortable your audience will be. So psych yourself up and know that you have something worthwhile to offer. Look confident. Nothing is more deadly to a performance than embarrassing the audience and making them uneasy because you look like you're going to fall to pieces in front of their eyes. Put people at ease by showing them you know what you're doing. If you project a sense of enjoyment in what you do, you'll find the audience will support you and respond with appreciation.

Make eye contact with your audience

When insecure, many singers close their eyes. It's a natural way to hide and pretend "I'm not really here." When you close your eyes, though, you close off an important communication device — and performance *is* communication, above all else. *Look* at your audience.

Don't apologize for yourself

Inexperienced performers often make the mistake of giving excuses before they start. Don't say "I usually sound better but I have a cold today" or "My fingers are sore" or "I just learned the song and don't really know the words yet." In like manner, if you make a mistake on your guitar or sing the wrong verse to a song, let it go by. Chances are, no one will notice anyway, and bringing it to everyone's attention by a facial expression or a remark will only throw you off and make the audience doubt your abilities.

Take command of your audience

When you have the stage and the microphone, *you* are the person in charge. Go on-stage knowing that both you and your audience are going to have a good time. (Tell yourself that if they don't enjoy themselves, it's their problem, not yours.) Take command, and give them everything you've got.

by Debbi Fields

As a little girl, I didn't know that I would go into the cookie business, but there was always a guiding force: I knew that whatever I did, it would be something where I could watch people smile. I began baking when I was thirteen years old, and whenever someone took a bite of my cookies, I saw a big smile on their face.

Debbi Fields began with what some people considered a "half-baked" idea for a store entirely devoted to cookies and turned it into an American success story. Mrs. Fields' Cookies now has more than seven hundred stores across the United States and in six foreign countries.

When I was twenty, I decided it was time to think about what I wanted to do for the rest of my life. My father had always told me, "Do something you love." For me, that was baking cookies. As I built up Mrs. Fields' Cookies, I learned some secrets for starting a successful business. They can help whether you're starting a lemonade stand, a dog-walking service, or some bigger business venture.

Choose something you love to do. By focusing on something you really enjoy, you're much more likely to succeed. It should be something that you'd spend your free time doing anyway. Because I loved to bake all the time, my cookies got better and better. This success made me enjoy baking even more. One reinforced the other.

The greatest failure is not to try. Even though I had no business experience, I decided to open the first Mrs. Fields' Cookies store about sixteen years ago. Everyone I encountered said things like, "Oh, you can't do that. You'll fail. That's a stupid idea. Don't try." People don't like to venture into the unknown. But trying an unknown enterprise means that you're getting ready to learn something new.

I kept reminding myself that the greatest failure was not to try. And even if I didn't succeed, trying would be better than doing nothing.

Try anything...and everything. After my store was open, I waited for customers to come and buy my cookies. And I waited...and waited. Hours passed, but nobody came into my store. It was depressing! It looked as though what everybody had told me was true: I was unsuccessful, nobody would buy my cookies, I was going to fail. So I said to myself, "Well, I can't just sit here and watch this happen. I have to try something. Not trying is simply asking for failure."

That's when I took a sheet of cookies and marched up and down the street, stopping people and offering them samples. Some of them came back to my store and bought cookies—and the rest, as they say, is history. What did the trick is the unconventional wisdom that if one thing doesn't work, you have to keep trying new ideas until something does stick. You never want to close the book on your dreams and think, "Oh, if only I had tried this, or done that!" Try everything. Sure, you might fail; maybe it just wasn't meant to be. But at least you'll know in your heart of hearts that you gave it your very best shot.

Don't go into business just to make money. I've heard lots of people say, "I want to make a million dollars." They go into business only for money, rather than to provide a product or service they absolutely love. This is a mistake. Unless they find something they're passionate about, they'll never make it.

In life you have to understand what's most valuable. When I was growing up, my father used to say to me, "True wealth is family and friends." He was right.

After you've got your business started, follow these guidelines for running it successfully.

Don't ask anyone to do something you wouldn't do yourself. Be willing to do the hardest jobs, the ones nobody else wants. In my business it might be something like mopping the floors or putting things away. Once I went into one of my stores in San Diego, California, and the supplies had just arrived—sacks of flour, chocolate chips, butter, and so forth. The first thing I did was start putting it away. The employees said, "Stop, Debbi; don't *you* do that!" I said, "No, come on; we're a team." I'm a real believer that you create teams by working *together*. My success didn't come because of Debbi Fields, but because the people I worked with allowed me to succeed.

Look at your mistakes as chances to learn. Some of my biggest mistakes have also been the most educational. As an example, one day the state of California came to me and said I was violating state regulations by having eighteen-year-olds clean the mixers in my stores. The state levied a heavy fine. I didn't know how I'd ever find the money to pay it. I went to see the judge, who said, "I understand that you didn't know the

Krispie Kandy Bar Cookies from Mrs. Fields' Kitchen

Ingredients:

2 cups all-purpose flour
1 cup quick oats (not instant)
1 teaspoon baking soda
¼ teaspoon salt
¾ cup brown sugar
¾ cup granulated sugar

1 cup butter (2 sticks) softened to room
   temperature (do not microwave)
2 eggs
2 teaspoons pure vanilla extract
10- to 12-ounce crispy-rice chocolate bar
   (broken into ½-inch chunks)

How to bake them:

Preheat oven to 300 degrees.

In a medium bowl, mix together the flour, oats, baking soda, and salt with a wire whisk. Set aside. With an electric mixer on medium speed, blend both sugars together in a large, deep bowl until they're the consistency of fluffy sand. Cut each stick of butter into four pieces and beat together with the sugars until creamy. Scrape down the sides of the bowl with a rubber spatula.

Add the eggs and vanilla, and beat on low speed until the mixture is fully blended. Add the flour-oat mixture and candy bar chunks. Mix on low speed until just blended. Do not overmix.

Form the cookies with a 1½-ounce ice cream scoop, or use a rounded table-spoon. Drop them onto an ungreased cookie sheet, spacing them 2 inches apart. Bake in the oven for 20 to 22 minutes. They are done when the edges turn golden and the cookies spring back when touched. Don't brown them. Immediately transfer the cookies to a cool surface.

Yields: 30 three-inch cookies.

regulations, but that doesn't excuse you." Right then, I realized that you need to spend time learning every aspect of your business. You can't afford to be ignorant. Getting my hand slapped taught me a valuable lesson, and it's a good thing it happened when I had only a few stores. What if it had happened when I had seven hundred stores? I'd probably have been fined right out of business.

It's amazing but true that some things you think are horrible actually end up to be a blessing. I've always believed that life teaches us in a way that sometimes looks like a negative, but generally always turns out to be a positive.

There may come a time when you want to expand your business—open a second store, add employees, buy more equipment, and so forth. Here are a few guidelines.

"No" is not an acceptable answer when seeking financing. "Financing" is the money needed to start or expand a business, and it's usually obtained from a bank. When I was starting out, I went to bank after bank. They'd listen to my plans (and eat all the cookies I brought) and then say no. I told myself, "I know there's somebody out there who wants to say yes. I just have to find them!" That gave me the courage to keep knocking on doors, even when people shut the doors in my face. I couldn't stop, because the day I stopped searching meant that my dream would never be realized. I just don't believe in giving up.

You must have command of your business. A lot of people want to expand, but they don't have their first business running steadily yet. In particular, you need to know all the costs involved in your business, because they're going to multiply as you grow.

Find enthusiastic employees. Surround yourself with people who love the product or service as much as you do. Let's say you have a dog-grooming business. Find people who *love* dogs and enjoy taking care of them.

Provide excellent training. I think that training should go on every day, and I've always viewed myself as a teacher. I never say to someone, "Do this." Instead, I explain *why*. For instance, our stores never sell a cookie that's more than two hours out of the oven. (The resulting "cookie orphans" are donated to charity.) It's not that the cookies self-destruct after two hours or taste awful. It's just that I always want to have fresh cookies coming out of the oven, because the most important thing we offer is the experience that a warm cookie creates. When I ask employees what happens when they serve a warm cookie, they tell me, "The customer says 'Mmmmm!'" The employees realize that the two-hour limit isn't just a silly rule, but part of a philosophy of doing business.

Actually, I don't see myself as being in the cookie business. My job is to generate a smile, and it just happens to come in the form of a cookie. I hope *you* will find a way to spread smiles in your life and business, too.

Mrs. Fields' Baking "Doughs and Don'ts"

Making dough

■ Do start with the freshest, purest ingredients available—fresh butter, real vanilla extract, nothing artificial or imitation.

■ Don't use a microwave to melt your butter or margarine, because this creates dark, flat, greasy cookies. Just allow the butter or margarine to warm up to room temperature.

■ Don't overmix the dough, which can make it runny and produce tough cookies. If the dough is too soft, chill it in the refrigerator for 20 minutes.

Baking

■ Don't use dark pans, which tend to burn the bottoms of the cookies. Instead, use shiny aluminum cookie sheets.

■ Do drop cookie dough with an ice cream scoop to make perfectly sized and shaped cookies.

■ Do cool the cookie sheets before dropping cookies, to prevent spreading.

■ Do use the "touch" method to know when your cookies are finished baking. If the cookie has spring to it, similar to cake, the cookie is perfect.

Cooling and storing

■ Do immediately transfer cookies from the cookie sheet to a cool surface.

■ Don't place cookies on a chopping block to cool. They may pick up the flavor of the garlic or onion you chopped for last night's dinner.

■ Do store cookies in an airtight container with a piece of bread (which helps the cookies stay soft).

■ Don't refrigerate cookies. Freeze them in an airtight bag while they're still fresh and reheat or thaw at room temperature when you're ready to eat them.

How to Play Polo on an Elephant

by Barnaby Conrad

Barnaby Conrad has fought bulls, boxed at college, and also wrestled with a man-eating typewriter to produce twenty-five books, including the best-selling *Matador* and *Hemingway's Spain*.

The way you play polo on an elephant is just like the way you play it on horseback, only you need either a short elephant or a very long mallet. You also need seven other people with elephants. They probably don't live on your block, so you must travel to Nepal, a small country located next door to India.

The maharajahs of India started the game of elephant polo a long time ago, but recently more and more foreigners have found the fun of playing. It's not taken terribly seriously, except by a few hundred dedicated polo players (and the elephants). The players meet every year in December for a three-day contest held near Katmandu, Nepal. Towering all around the polo field are the highest mountains in the world, the Himalayas, covered in snow. But it's sunny and warm down where the players are.

Elephant polo is a colorful event because the elephants have their faces and sides painted with bright designs. The game is played like regular polo, with four players on a team who try to hit the ball between goal posts at each end of the field. You might think elephant polo would be very dangerous, but it isn't because of one important fact: The elephant is very aware of his own strength and bulk, and he avoids physical contact with the other elephants at all costs. This is very good for the player on top of the elephant.

An elephant takes a lot of guiding, so a man called a *ma-*

hout, or trainer, sits behind the elephant's ears. He guides the elephant with his knees and with an *anka,* which is a metal rod with a hook on the end. It looks ferocious to us, but it doesn't hurt the elephant's thick hide the way it would our tender skin. The player—that's you—sits literally lashed to a blanket saddle on top of the elephant, behind the mahout.

The game is played with long-handled mallets and a real polo ball. For a while they decided to play with a large soccer ball instead, but the elephants took such delight in squashing the soccer balls that the players went back to regulation wooden balls. Elephants are extraordinarily intelligent, much more than horses, and they seem to understand what the point of the contest is—following the ball and getting into the best position for the man to swing his mallet. They never pick up the ball with their trunk, which they can do easily, until the end of the game.

The best elephant polo players take a full swing with the mallet. The mallet goes in a 360-degree circle. But a beginner would do well not to try that. Instead, play more as though it were croquet, and tap-tap-tap the ball down the field. This is because the chance of missing the ball entirely is so great when you take a big swing. During the game I played in Nepal I thought I'd really show them, so I took

> ## How to Mount an Elephant
>
> **Ask the elephant to kneel down. (If it won't do this, ask the elephant trainer to ask the elephant.) Grab hold of the elephant's tail. Now step on the heel of a back leg and pull yourself up the rump of the animal. This is the most difficult part of the whole game of elephant polo—getting aboard!**
>
> **When you want to get off again, the elephant sags down in the front, his rear legs go back behind him, and you slide off easily.**

huge swings. Most of the time I missed the ball. My wife, Mary, simply tapped the ball down the field and made the goal. (A lot of women play elephant polo, and there are women's teams made up mostly of English and American players, as well as Indians.)

The best elephant polo players are Sikhs, who come from India. They wear pink or white turbans on their heads and white jodhpurs (baggy pants). During my game I played goalee, and when I saw the Sikh team bearing down on me, it was really quite frightening. Those elephants go fast! They lumber along with that peculiar elephantine gait, but they can really move. I tried to stop the Sikhs, but of course I couldn't. They made four goals off me.

Nobody said elephant polo was an easy game—but it sure is fun!

Learn to Juggle the Easy Way!

by Dave Finnigan

Even if you think you're too klutzy, you'll soon be saying, "Look, Ma—I'm juggling!" The secret is simple: Learn to juggle with nylon scarves. Compared to balls or oranges, scarves move at a leisurely pace and have lots of "hang time," so you can juggle in what seems like slow motion. (These scarves can be found at magic stores, which often carry juggling equipment. Or get filmy chiffon material at a fabric shop, and cut it into three 18-inch squares.)

Most people think that when you juggle, you've got to throw three things in the air all at once. But often there's just one object in the air, sometimes two—never three. So juggling is a lot easier than it looks. To learn the basic "cascade" pattern, let's take it step by step.

Tips and Tricks

- Scarf juggling is gentle and flowing, so just take your time.
- Don't think while you juggle; thinking takes too much time. Instead, use your body and your senses to feel the pattern that the scarves should be making.
- Once you've got the basics down pat, go ahead and try some fancy stuff, like throwing a scarf behind your back or under your leg. When you're ready, move on to juggling with balls and other objects. You can do a hilarious routine with three rubber chickens. Don't be afraid to try anything!
- If you drop something while people are watching you, don't worry; they may think it's all part of the act. You can cover up your flub with a funny line: "Whoops—a sudden gust of gravity!" Or say something tongue-in-cheek, like "Hmm...almost dropped one." That's called showmanship.

First scarf

Dave Finnigan has taught 500,000 people to juggle. He wrote *The Complete Juggler,* a textbook on the art. He also runs Jugglebug, a company in Edmonds, Washington, that makes and sells juggling scarves, balls, rings, and clubs. He advises that juggling equipment is sold at magic stores everywhere.

a) Hold a scarf in the middle, and let it hang like a "ghost."

b) Swing your arm across your chest and up high.

c) Release the scarf; your palm faces outward, as if you were waving goodbye.

d) With the other hand, catch the scarf.

e) Claw downward like a tiger.

f) Raise that arm and swing it across your chest the other way.

When you can do the figure eight without any trouble…

g) Catch the scarf with the opposite hand, clawing downward.

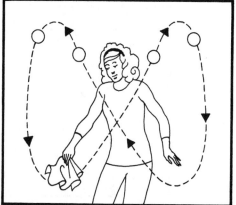

h) Repeat over and over, throwing across and catching downward. The scarf traces a path that looks like a figure eight turned on its side.

Add a second scarf

a) Grasp a scarf in each hand.

b) Throw the first scarf across. When it reaches the top and starts to fall, keep your eye on it and...

The rhythm is: throw-throw-catch-catch.

c) Throw the second scarf across in the other direction. (Your hands trace an "X" across your chest.)

d) Catch the first scarf, moving your hand straight down; then catch the second scarf the same way. Now add a third scarf...

Juggle all three scarves

a) Hold two of the scarves in one hand. Grip the first by pressing your fingers against your palm. Hold the second between the tips of the thumb and forefinger; you'll throw this one first.

b) Toss the first scarf. When it starts to fall, throw the second scarf from your other hand.

c) As your hand comes down from throwing number two, it catches number one.

d) When the second scarf peaks, toss the third; it follows the same path as the first one did.

e) As your hand comes down from throwing the third scarf, it catches the second. Now your other hand throws number four—which is actually number one coming around again.

f) Keep alternating your hands—right, left, right, left. Every time one scarf gets to the top, throw another, then catch the one that's in the air. Hey look, you're juggling!

A Two-Headed, Four-Legged Juggling Creature

a) You and a friend can juggle scarves together. Stand side by side. One person holds two scarves, the other has one. The person with two scarves begins.

b) Each person uses only one hand. You're like some strange, juggling creature with two hands—and two heads!

How to Get in *The Guinness Book of World Records*

by Ashrita Furman

About one-quarter of the records in *The Guinness Book of World Records* are broken each year. That's bad news for me, because if I want to hold my ten records, I have to beat every new challenger! But it's good news for you, because you have lots of chances to set a new record. You'll feel a real sense of accomplishment if you set a world record in anything, and seeing your name in the Guinness book is great fun.

Some of the categories are wacky, like spitting a watermelon seed for distance (the record is 68 feet, 9 $\frac{1}{8}$ inches). Some are unusual, like amassing the world's largest ball of string (the winning ball is almost 13 feet across and weighs 11 tons). Some categories are very hard, like somersaulting. I set the record by somersaulting 12.25 miles along the route of Paul Revere's famous ride in Massachusetts. Guinness rules forbid stopping along the way; they allow you to throw up, and that's about it. So a challenger has to overcome dizziness and nausea, exhaustion and pain. I did 8,341 somersaults.

I'm thirty-nine years old, but I consider myself a big kid, and my records are all for kid stuff—pogo-sticking for distance, playing hopscotch, walking 70 miles with a full bottle of milk balanced on my head, "joggling" (running and juggling at the same time), and that sort of thing. I've learned a few tricks for setting world records, and I hope they'll help you get in to the Guinness book, too.

The holder of ten Guinness titles, New Yorker Ashrita Furman is unique in the field of world records. No one else has set more Guinness records in different categories— from doing jumping jacks to yodeling, from pogo-sticking up Mount Fuji to juggling underwater.

Choose a category that's already in the book

If you invent your own category, Guinness probably won't accept the record. They have only a certain amount of space, and if a new record goes in, another one has to come out.

Look through the book until you find a category that appeals to you. That's how I settled on trying to break the yodeling record. I'm not even a singer, and I drove my friends crazy trying to learn to yodel. Finally, I yodeled for 27 hours straight and set the record. It went into the Guinness book.

Another time, however, I pogo-sticked up the stairs in the tallest tower in the world, the CN Tower in Toronto. British television filmed it, and we hoped that Guinness would accept the feat. But it did not because there was no category for it. So remember: Picking a category that's already in the book gives you a much better chance.

If you *do* have an idea for a new category, be sure to write or telephone the Guinness office first (see box). The editors will say whether they'll consider it. If you tell them, "I'm going to see how many times I can stick out my tongue in ten hours," or "I'm going to bang my head against a wall one hundred thousand times," they'll probably say no. (Obviously, you shouldn't do anything

---

Getting in Touch with Guinness

To obtain the rules for breaking records in each category, to verify current world records, or to ask for other information, mail your request (with a stamped, self-addressed envelope) to:

Facts on File
460 Park Avenue South
New York, NY 10016

or telephone:
Guinness Line (212) 447-5864
(Leave a message on the machine, and someone will call you back. The number rings in New York City.)

dangerous or harmful!) But when I telephoned to propose pogo-sticking for distance, they said: "Well, it sounds like a good category. We can't promise to put it in the book, but go ahead and submit it." It helps if the stunt creates a lot of interest—which means *competition* from other challengers who submit claims in the same category.

And there's always a chance. Once I invented something called "land rowing," when I mounted an indoor rowing machine on wheels. Today land rowing is a Guinness category, and the current record holder rowed across the entire United States! Recently I thought up "gluggling," or juggling underwater. I put on a scuba tank, climbed into a tank of water, and juggled for 57 minutes. It's a new category, so I'm waiting to see whether Guinness will accept it.

Pick a category you enjoy

If the stunt won't give you some joy, forget about it. A big part of setting a Guinness world record is to have a lot of fun!

Know the rules

Fortunately, there are printed rules for every category, which you can get by writing or telephoning Guinness to ask for them (see box). Without knowing the rules, you could be eliminated on a technicality. When I went for the yodeling record, for instance, the rules allowed a five-minute rest *after* each hour of yodeling. If I'd yodeled for 55 minutes and then taken a five-minute rest, I'd have been disqualified.

Find out what the current record is

Records printed in the Guinness book may not be the very latest ones. Records are broken all the time, and claims come in after the book is published. Be sure to call the Guinness office *the day before* you try to break the record. As an example of what can happen if you don't, I went for the record in the wall press category, which involves sitting against a wall as if you were sitting in a chair—but there's no chair. It's torture! Most people can do it for three to five minutes. The record was four hours and 45 minutes. I trained until I was ready to break it, but when I phoned the Guinness editors, they said they'd just received a claim from a man in India who had done the wall press for 10½ hours. What if I hadn't telephoned? I'd have done the wall press for maybe six grueling hours, and my record wouldn't have counted. It would have been horrible.

Train by actually doing the stunt

If you plan to go for the record in jumping jacks, do a thousand of them, then two thousand the next time, then three thousand, and so on. It's good to do other exercises to keep in shape, but be sure to *concentrate* on the event in which you're trying to break the record.

Plan ahead

Prepare as much as you possibly can. Think of everything that can go wrong. Then go on a trial run. I should have done this when I went for the record for deep-knee bends. Doing them in a gym is so boring that I hatched the idea of going up in a hot-air balloon. It turned out that the whole balloon dipped whenever I did a knee-bend, so I was fighting the motion of the balloon every time. Breaking that record was really tough. I should have given it a try beforehand.

Expect the unexpected

Because things can never be planned perfectly, *something* will go wrong. When it does, you can't think: "Well, this isn't going to work. I didn't expect this to happen, so I'll have to stop and try again sometime." You have to go with the flow, as they say. Once I tried for the "joggling" record by running a marathon as I juggled. For the last seven miles I had a bug in my eye! There was no way to get it out, since I was juggling and didn't have a free hand. I just had to keep going.

Another time, when I started out on my land rowing record, I crashed after a few minutes and the machine got stuck in gear. I couldn't fix it, so I had to go the whole distance in the hardest gear. Actually, that setback inspired me somehow, because it was more of a challenge. There are times when you can turn an obstacle into an opportunity.

Make things easier on yourself

You can find ways to give yourself a break and still stay within the Guinness rules. In the hand clapping category, the claps have to be audible at 120 yards. I first tried to break the record in New York City at Lincoln Center, which is really noisy. Even

though I clapped my hands as loud as I could, the witnesses could barely hear me. After fifteen hours I had to stop. I wondered how I could make things easier on myself the next time. Then I remembered that sound carries well over water, so I went to a pond. I clapped at one end and seated the witnesses at the other end. Guinness approved this plan. (Be sure to check with them ahead of time.) It was easier on me, and it didn't break any rules.

Another secret is to bring along a few friends to encourage you and offer advice. I remember that the night before I set the somersaulting record, I ate four slices of pizza. (I was doing something called "carbo loading," which increases your athletic energy.) The undigested pizza was sloshing around in my stomach, and I felt really sick. A friend who came along finally convinced me to drink some pure Coca-Cola syrup, which overcomes nausea. I wasn't thinking very clearly after somersaulting for miles, so my friend's suggestion really saved me.

Provide all the proof that Guinness requires

Guinness can't send editors all over the world to verify it when people set new records, so you have to prove it to them. First, you need two witnesses. They can't be your friends; they must be people of standing in the community, like a school principal and a policeman, so Guinness will know that they're reliable and wouldn't lie. Also, you need an official logbook, which the witnesses have to sign at certain intervals. (When you ask Guinness to send the rules for your category, they'll include details on setting up your logbook.) You must do the stunt in a public place and provide a sheet of paper for passersby to sign their names, addresses, and the date. Also, be sure to send Guinness a photograph of yourself taken during your successful attempt.

Finally, you need media coverage to confirm your record. That's one reason why I do stunts in unusual ways or unusual places, so a newspaper reporter or a TV cameraman will show up. Once I pogo-sticked up Mount Fuji in Japan. The Japanese loved it, and I got national press coverage.

Learn concentration

Feats like juggling require a lot of concentration, and even the boring ones (like clapping) demand that you pay attention to one thing for a long time. A very simple exercise is to look at something—a flower, a picture, or any object—and try to think only of that. Even within three minutes you'll find that your mind wanders all over the place. As soon as it does, bring it back to that object. Practice every day. Once you get to three minutes, then go to five and then to ten minutes. When you can focus on something for ten minutes, you're doing very well. That kind of concentration can help you set a Guinness record.

If you do get in the book, you'll feel a great sense of accomplishment. That's why I do these crazy things. Going for a world record is a wonderful challenge, and the person you challenge really isn't the individual who holds the current record—it's *yourself.* Never give up!

Float Off to Sleep on a Pink Cloud

by Lilias Folan

For the past twenty years, Lilias Folan has taught yoga to millions of viewers on public television. She also produces yoga videos and audiotapes, including a complete course called *Rest, Relax, and Sleep.*

The little things you do before bedtime can help ease you into a heavenly night's sleep. Closing the bedroom door, pulling down the window shade, playing some quiet music, and thinking peaceful and kind thoughts—these things can help us relax and go to sleep.

I teach yoga, a wonderful system from India for keeping your body and mind full of energy, yet relaxed. Part of yoga is exercising and stretching your body; part is relaxing your mind and visualizing good things. First I'll explain a little about visualization and relaxation, then I'll discuss how these tools can send you sailing away to a sweet sleep.

Visualization is seeing a picture in your mind. The trick is to let an image (a picture) come to you like a daydream. Try it. Close your eyes. Look to an imaginary movie screen behind your forehead. Now remember what a lemon looks like…its color…its shape…its texture. Smell the lemon. Even take a bite of it, and taste the sour juice. That's visualization!

Now for relaxation. The trick is to feel it, to feel your body growing quiet and restful. During the Pink Cloud Relaxation (see below), take your time. Feel as light as a feather…as if you don't weigh anything…you're floating. Remember, relaxation is a feeling!

To do the Pink Cloud Relaxation, you (or your mom or dad) should speak the words that follow into a tape recorder. Read in an easygoing, gentle voice. Be sure to pause for a few moments at the ellipses (...), and to take longer pauses of ten to sixty seconds when you see this: (*wait*).

Later, when you climb into bed, you can turn on your tape recorder, listen to the Pink Cloud Relaxation, and just float away to sleep.

Pink Cloud Relaxation

Sit at the edge of your bed, raise your arms over your head, and do a lazy stretch and a big yawn. Be sure to raise both arms over your head, and make a big yawning sound!

Now get under the covers...lie down...uncross your ankles ...rest your arms along your sides. Close your eyes. You can take your time...and watch yourself breathe...watch your chest rise and fall...just like you'd watch a butterfly on a flower (*wait*).

Now take a moment to let your day go. Imagine that you're placing your worries and problems in a great big basket (*wait*). After you've put them all in the basket...notice that the basket is tied to a hot air balloon...see the bright colors of the balloon. Imagine the balloon lifting off, carrying the basket full of your cares and worries into the sky...far...far away...maybe behind the big moon. And for tonight, leave the basket there... knowing that, in the morning, you can get the basket back if you really want to (*wait*).

Once again, now, daydream...everyone daydreams...remember a day when the blue sky was wide open...big... clear...not a cloud in the sky. See it on the movie screen behind your forehead (*wait*). Now notice in the distance…far, far away …there's a tiny pink dot in the pure blue sky. See this tiny dot slowly coming nearer to you…closer…closer…to form a fluffy pink cloud. The color pink is soothing and inviting…you can almost feel the cloud calling you…to come and lie down… come and rest on it like a soft pink pillow. Now, because it looks so inviting, you quietly lie down on your back on this safe, soft, pink mist…so warm. A smile comes to your mouth…you enjoy how this cloud feels. The pink mist is safely holding up your head and neck…the curve of your back…it lifts your arms and elbows…feel them floating (*wait*). Feel the pink mist under your legs…lifting the hollows of your knees…supporting your heels. You feel so light…safe…your whole body, light as a feather…floating (*wait*).

You are relaxing…floating…on the warm pink cloud… there's a smile of enjoyment on your face…as you continue floating…safely on the pink cloud (*wait*).

Now…slowly…come back to your regular weight…the corners of your mouth turn up a little…you feel wonderful…refreshed…contented (*wait*). Drift off into restful…wonderful …sleep…

Ten Ways to Calm a Crying Baby

by Diana S. Greene

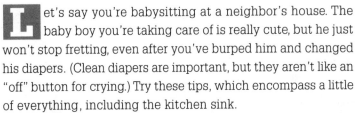et's say you're babysitting at a neighbor's house. The baby boy you're taking care of is really cute, but he just won't stop fretting, even after you've burped him and changed his diapers. (Clean diapers are important, but they aren't like an "off" button for crying.) Try these tips, which encompass a little of everything, including the kitchen sink.

1. Food. Babies need to eat more often than older kids or adults, who can live on just three meals a day, plus snacks. First try feeding the baby a bottle, even if he had one half an hour ago. Babies can be big consumers on certain days, and you might just be babysitting on one of them.

2. Pacifier. Ahh, the baby's rubber buddy! Don't leave home without it! Some babies have a huge need to suck. The pacifier has been made popular in "The Simpsons" by little Maggie, who is a realistic portrait of what babies are like. Often they just need something to plug them up.

3. Baby swing. Motion in general really helps a child who's fussy or colicky. If the house happens to have one of those wind-up baby swings, give it a try. Or maybe there's a swing outside, or a hammock, where you can hold the baby close to your body (babies need a lot of physical contact) and give him a little gentle swinging.

4. Rocking chair. Another way to get a baby moving is in a rocking chair. Before he was born he spent nine months just enjoying the gentle motion inside his mom's belly, and he

Diana S. Greene is the author of *79 Ways to Calm a Crying Baby.* She got the idea for the book from taking care of her oldest child, "who now cries only when she hurts herself, like most kids." Formerly a journalist for Cable News Network (CNN), Diana Greene teaches creative writing at schools in Arizona.

needs to continue with that movement. It really can settle him down.

As you're rocking, the baby may fall asleep. Sometimes a crying baby is just overtired and needs to be calmed down before going to bed.

5. Kitchen sink. Here's a nice, simple (but dull for you) method to soothe a tearful infant. A lot of babies respond well to some kind of "white noise"—a dull wash of sound, like the gentle hum made by an electric fan. Stand next to the sink or bathtub with the baby in your arms, and turn on the tap. Running water gives babies something they can listen to and look at, and somehow it appeases their hostilities. You may feel kind of stupid just standing there with the water running, but it really did the trick with my first baby.

6. Vacuum cleaner. This method sounds strange, too, but it works because a vacuum cleaner also produces white noise. Younger babies especially like to be immersed in this noise, so if you feel desperate, turn on the vacuum cleaner and see what happens. (You can even vacuum the house and earn some points with the people you're babysitting for!)

7. Bouncing on the bed. This is a great technique, but you do need to be very careful. Take off your shoes and stand in the middle of the bed. Hold the baby close to your chest with both hands, and very gently jump up and down. (Don't get carried away and try for a big bounce, as if you were going to do a flip on a trampoline.) You don't even need to lift your feet up, just your heels, so you get a little spring. This method worked wonders with my baby, although my mother thought it was preposterous. You can even hum along, and then you're like a one-man band!

8. Stroll. If you are in a safe neighborhood and it's all right to go outside, strolling a fussy baby can be very helpful. (Just make sure you fasten his seat belt in the stroller.) Going for an outing offers movement, lots of noises, and new scenery; if you have a discontented baby who demands a full stage of entertainment, these should take care of the problem. It's also nice for *you* to get out of the house. Sometimes being inside with a crying baby can make the house shrink to a horribly small size.

9. Sing. Try out your own lungs to compete with the baby's lung power! When my baby cried, I sang a lot of songs, even though I'm not exactly Whitney Houston. A baby feels very comforted by hearing a voice next to him. And if you're holding the baby, he can feel the vibration of your voice—that's how he heard his mother—and I think babies like to harken back to a time when everything was taken care of.

If you can't remember the words to songs, just turn on the radio and sing along. Or sing "Happy Birthday" over and over. A baby really isn't fussy about the tune you select. If you get inspired, dance a little. That will combine sound, touch, and movement—and very often a tearful baby needs the whole shebang.

10. The great outdoors. Being taken outdoors can be very beneficial to a baby. Show him around! Look at a plant, a chair, an animal. Let him enjoy the fresh air. Spending time outdoors is also very calming to the babysitter, who is going to feel stress whenever a baby cries.

Here's a general rule I learned with my own first baby: If everything you do fails to make a baby stop crying, always stay calm. If you start to get tense yourself, that can make the baby more tense, and you may find yourself in a big struggle that could be avoided simply by putting the baby into the crib and taking a ten-minute break. (Maybe you can go watch the water in the kitchen sink!) People who are responsible for a little kid, such as parents and babysitters, don't realize that sometimes they need to take a break themselves if things aren't working out.

When you babysit a tearful child, you'll be busy. You may have to forget about doing your homework. You'll really earn your money the night you sit for that child. But you'll feel great when you succeed in calming him down and making him happy.

Play "Killer" Table Tennis

by Larry Hodges

Most people call this game Ping-Pong (a brand name), but serious players call it table tennis. These tips will help you outsmash, outspin, and outserve your opponents.

Larry Hodges has been ranked among the top 30 players in the U.S. (out of 7,000 players) and is the author of *Table Tennis: Steps to Success.* Formerly the manager of the table tennis program at the Olympic Training Center in Colorado Springs, he is now the national coaching chairman of the U.S. Table Tennis Association and director of the National Table Tennis Center in Maryland.

Proper equipment

About 90 percent of the top players use a racket with a smooth rubber surface that has sponge underneath. These rackets "grip" the ball, making it easier to put a spin on the ball. (Don't use a hard rubber racket, because the ball pops off with no spin.) It's also fine to use a racket with little rubber nubs on the surface (called "pips out"), but be sure there is a layer of sponge underneath.

Grip

Grip the racket as if you were shaking hands. Your little, fourth, and middle fingers wrap around the handle. Your index finger extends along the blade, or flat part of the paddle, on one side; your thumb lies along the other side. These two fingers are placed at the bottom of the blade, not on the playing surface, so they won't get in the way of the ball.

Stance

Don't stand rooted to the ground like a tree; instead, move to the ball. The reason is simple: All shots are different. If you stand still and reach for them, you must hit the ball differently

each time, and your returns will be irregular. But if you move to the ball, you'll be able to hit it the exact same way every time. Then your returns will be strong and unfailing.

As for position, stand a little to the left of the center line (if you're a right-handed player). You should cover half the table with your forehand and half with your backhand. Or you can slightly favor your forehand. Beginners often get in the habit of playing too much backhand, which is a weaker and less adaptable stroke than forehand.

Smashes

There are many kinds of smashes. If someone hits you a high ball, you should know how to plaster it back at him with your forehand (see "How to Smash a High Ball"). But you should also be able to smash with your backhand.

When a player misses a smash, the ball usually goes off the far end of the table. To prevent this, aim low by tilting your racket downward and stroking from behind the ball. This works better than just aiming straight down at the opponent's side of the table (a shot that often sends the ball sailing off the other end, because it adds backspin that lifts the ball).

Spins

You put spin on a Ping-Pong ball by grazing it with your racket. There are three types of spins: backspin, topspin, and sidespin. To hit the ball hard and fast at someone in a rally, put a light topspin on the ball; this makes the ball drop, or sink, so it won't go off the end of the table. (You automatically get some topspin if you hold your racket tilted downward as you stroke.) Backspin is good for defensive shots. The ball is easier for you to control, because it moves more slowly, and backspin makes the ball travel in a straight line, so you can aim it exactly where you want it. You also can keep the ball low more easily, so it won't bounce up and give your opponent a chance to smash it. Sidespin in a rally is for advanced players.

You can also put spin on serves. A topspin serve often forces the other person to return the ball high, because the ball jumps upward off his racket. (Do a topspin serve by grazing the ball upward as you stroke it.) A backspin serve often makes the other player hit the ball down into the net. (See "A Tricky Backspin Serve.") A sidespin serve jumps off the other person's racket and flies to the side. If the return doesn't sail right off the table, it will often go to the place where you want it—for instance, to your strong forehand side. (For this, graze the ball sideways to your right as you serve.)

How to Smash a High Ball

Note: Directions are for right-handers; left-handers should reverse "left" and "right."

1. Move into position to use your forehand.
2. Place your right foot back and to the right of your left foot.
3. Turn your shoulders and waist to the right.
4. Put most of your weight on your back foot.
5. Keep the hitting surface of your racket angled slightly downward.
6. Bring the racket straight backward.
7. Raise the racket to a point directly behind where it will contact the ball.
8. Push forward off your back foot.
9. Throw your upper body and arm into the shot as the ball reaches its highest point.
10. Plaster the ball!

To defend against spin serves, adjust your return to counteract the spin. If your opponent serves with topspin, for example, aim for the net or even lower. To return a backspin serve, aim the ball high and perhaps put backspin on it yourself by tilting your racket upward and making contact underneath the ball to lift it over the net. To return a sidespin serve, just aim in the direction opposite to the spin.

Fast serves

A fast serve robs the other player of time to react, so he blows the shot. (However, if he reacts fast enough, he can use your own speed against you on the return.) One key to a fast serve is topspin, which brings the ball down so it won't miss the table. It will have the most time to come down if you have the ball bounce very near the endline on both sides. Serve so the ball travels as low as possible, making it harder to return.

Winning strategy

Play aggressively, but also consistently. Use speed or spin to keep attacking the ball. However, if you *always* try to plaster the ball, you'll make too many mistakes. Learn how hard you can hit any given shot and still get it on the table every time.

Even if you have one great serve that the other player will probably miss ten times during a game, don't use it ten times in a row. Your opponent could miss it five times, then learn how to return it and never miss again, so you'd only get five points out of the serve, instead of ten.

Hit the ball to one of three spots:

1. Your opponent's weakest side. But don't overdo it, or he'll know what's coming.

2. Your opponent's wide backhand or wide forehand side. There's a lot of distance between these two corners of the table, and if the other player has to keep moving back and forth between them, he'll be hitting a lot of shots when he's off balance. Another advantage of playing to the corners is that you have the most room for your shot to hit the table. A Ping-Pong table is 9 feet long, but measures 10.3 feet from corner to corner. The extra distance gives you a real advantage.

A Tricky Backspin Serve

1. Hold your racket with its face tilted upward.

2. Bring your wrist back as far as you can, until the racket points almost backward.

3. Throw the ball up in the air, let it drop onto your racket, and then snap the racket forward and downward, so it grazes the *bottom* of the ball. The more you graze the ball, the more spin you'll get. (To do this serve well, your racket has to be almost underneath the ball, but while you're learning the serve, you'll have to contact more the back of the ball.) Your opponent will tend to return the ball into the net.

Hot tip: Wash the surface of your racket with water before you play. Rackets pick up dirt and grime that make the ball slip and cut the amount of spin. Tests show that washing the racket can actually double the spin you put on the ball, especially on the serve.

3. The elbow of your opponent's playing arm. This spot falls midway between his forehand and backhand, and in this situation most players feel indecisive about which stroke to use. The delay messes them up. They also have to move their whole body to get out of the way and into position — either to the left to hit a forehand return, or to the right for a backhand.

To return an aggressive elbow shot, follow this general rule: Use backhand if you are very close to the table, and forehand if you are not. A backhand is an easier shot to do quickly, because you're generally square to the table and don't have to move much. Forehand works well if you're already standing back from the table, because you have a little more time and room for your backswing.

These tips should get you started. Table tennis is now an Olympic sport. Maybe I'll see you playing at the Games!

For More Information:

Learn about joining the United States Table Tennis Association (USTTA) by phoning toll-free: 1-800-326-8788. They will send you free information about membership and clubs, coaches, and tournaments in your area.

Stage a Fake Fight like a Movie Stuntman

by Loren Janes

Stuntmen have always done fake fights. In old western movies and TV shows, there were plenty of knock-down, drag-out battles with bare fists. Today's martial arts movies have karate chops and fancy spinning kicks. But the actors never *really* get hit. I'll explain how stuntmen do fake fights, but I don't want you to try it with your friends. It's not safe. Stuntmen are professional athletes; but if *you* try to throw a fake punch, you could knock someone's teeth out. The fun is just knowing how it's done.

Stuntmen plan every detail of a movie fight long before they get to the BIFF!-POW!-BAM! stuff. It's laid out step by step, like a dance routine. They think everything through: If someone throws a punch that connects, what happens to the person getting hit? (A roundhouse punch would spin him to the right or left, for instance; a punch to the stomach would bend him over double.) Is the punch partially blocked, a full smash, or a glancing blow? These questions determine where the punch carries the person and also the next move that either fighter could make.

After the action is planned, making a fight look real depends on what we call camera angle—where the actors and camera are positioned. Movie film can't show the third dimension of depth; it's flat. This means I can throw a punch at your jaw and miss by eighteen inches, but on the screen it will look like a

In 1954 Loren Janes began his stunt career with a splash—an eighty-foot dive off a cliff at Catalina Island. Since then, he has appeared in more than five hundred movies and one thousand TV shows. He doubled for Steve McQueen during his entire career, as well as for Jack Nicholson, Paul Newman, and even Debbie Reynolds. A cofounder of the Stuntmen's Association of Motion Pictures and Television, he is a horseman, scuba diver, mountain climber, certified ski instructor, world traveler, and member of the Explorer's Club.

direct hit. Let's say the camera is focused over my shoulder at your face, and I throw a punch. The minute my fist crosses a direct imaginary line from the camera lens to your jaw, I've "hit" you. At least, to the camera it looks like a hit. (If the camera were placed to the side, it would see that I missed you by a mile.)

To make the punch look good, I'll use body English — I'll wind up, swing my shoulder, and add plenty of follow-through. But I could throw the greatest punch in the world, and if the other guy just stood there, it wouldn't look right. For the punch to look real, the other actor has to snap his head. A person's head will tend to move in the direction it is hit, but the head doesn't just stay there; it snaps back on its own. Some movie stars — John Wayne, Steve McQueen, James Garner — learned to take all sorts of fake punches realistically, and their fights look great.

If a star doesn't perform his own fights, the director will film some close-ups of the actor's face. When he edits the movie (puts together the various pieces of film later), he cuts from the fighting stuntman to the star's face and back again, and it will look like the actor is the one who's fighting.

To stage a fake fight, a stuntman has to understand the movie's characters. *Who* is fighting? If the hero is a hard-boiled detective, he has probably been in fights and can handle himself. But a wimpy college professor, who has never fought, won't know what he's doing and would throw punches differently.

Another important consideration is *where* the characters will be. Will they be inside a house, where they could crash through a window and then wrestle around on the sidewalk? Or in a corral with horses that may get spooked and stampede?

And there's the plot to consider. Maybe a policeman shows up and the bad guy runs away, so the fight requires only a few quick punches. On the other hand, the whole movie may have been building toward a final showdown between the hero and the "heavy," so the fight is a life-and-death battle.

There's one last secret of making a movie fight look real. The guy who gets "hit" by a punch hides a capsule in his mouth, filled with red liquid. (It's like toothpaste with a peppermint taste.) When the actor bites down on it, he spits out "blood." SOCK! POW! OOOPH!

Being a Professional Stuntman

I've been doing this for nearly forty years and have never broken a bone. So I want you to understand that a professional stuntman is not a crazy person who will do anything for a buck or a thrill. (Those are the ones who get hurt.) Most top stuntmen were college or even world-class athletes and have great coordination and timing. They stay in peak shape. (I mountain-bike four miles every morning, get off and run five miles, and bike four miles back to my house. Then I climb a rope, do gymnastics, and swim half a mile.) Professional stuntmen don't drink, smoke, or use drugs. They know about camera angles, editing, and other technical sides of moviemaking. Most important, they stay cool when something goes wrong during the stunt—if the fire gets too big or the cattle really stampede. They save themselves *and* the scene. It takes a certain type of person to do all this, and that's why only 1 of every 15,000 men (and women) who come to Hollywood hoping to do stunts actually succeeds in the movie industry.

A Stuntman's Bag of Tricks

CAUTION: Do NOT try any of these stunts yourself. They are dangerous and for professionals only!

Breakaway chairs

When a cowboy in a barroom brawl gets hit with a chair, he doesn't get hurt. That's because the chair is made of light balsa wood, held together with nothing but glue and slivers of wood. Oddly enough, the harder you hit somebody with a breakaway chair, the easier it breaks and the less likely it will hurt him. (Hitting softly could injure the other stuntman. It's like holding a twig in your hands and bending it slowly; you have to use a lot of force before it finally snaps. But giving the twig a quick jerk will snap it easily.)

"Double" cars

When the script calls for a car chase, even the stars' cars have doubles—duplicates that look exactly the same. That way, if something goes wrong and a car gets smashed up, the director can bring in the double and keep filming while the first car is being fixed. A car chase may look wild and reckless, but everything is carefully planned. Preparing and filming it may take weeks, but in the movie it's all over in a couple of minutes.

Bullet hits

Under his shirt the stuntman wears a "squib"—a tiny explosive device with a "blood" sack attached. Wires run down his pant leg and across the floor to a special effects technician. When the gunshot goes off, the special effects man touches the wires together, firing the explosion and throwing fake blood all over the place. It looks like a bullet hit.

Of course, the stuntman has to flinch and react just as he would if a bullet actually hit him. If a slug hit his shoulder, it would spin him around. A .45-caliber bullet in the stomach would hit him like a sledgehammer, folding him over. A shotgun blast would blow him backwards. The stuntman tries to make it look real.

Ratchets, air rams

A ratchet is a rig designed to jerk the stuntman backwards when he gets "shot." Under his clothes he wears a heavy vest with a wire coming out the back and attached to a pulley system. This rig can pull him backwards through the air about 20 feet.

An air ram is used when a stuntman is running. He steps on a box, its lid flips up (powered by air pressure), and tosses him 30 feet through the air. The stuntman has to be careful to step on the box stiff-legged; if his knee is bent, the device will break his leg.

Being dragged by a horse

An outlaw in a western movie sometimes falls off his horse, but the stirrup catches his boot and he gets dragged on the ground. In the old days the stuntman had a release mechanism, so when he was worn out or if the horse's hooves started to hit him, he pushed the release and it would let him go. But what if he got knocked cold when he fell off? Then he couldn't operate the release. So everyone switched to the opposite method: The stuntman holds the release in his hand, and if he gets knocked out, his hand relaxes and the stirrup releases him.

I've been dragged down city streets, through scrub brush, and right into rivers. Sometimes it's possible to wear pads, but you get awfully beat up any-way. There's no comfortable way to be dragged by a horse! And any time you work with animals—whether it's riding a horse or fighting a lion—you must remember that *they* haven't read the script. Anything can happen.

Flying

The stuntman is hooked up to wires that are painted and don't show up on film, so he appears to be flying. In the Disney movie *The Absent-Minded Professor* we drove a "flying car;" actually, it was hanging on wires from a crane that swung it through space.

Catching on fire

The stuntman's clothes are fireproofed and protective material is worn under-neath—material similar to that worn by racecar drivers. The clothes are painted with a thick glue-like substance, which is what burns, not the stuntman's jacket and pants.

In a burning building, fire consumes all the air, so it is not possible to breathe when you're engulfed in flames. The solution is carrying a small bottle of air on your chest and breathing through a tube. The air lasts about six or seven minutes.

Falling off cliffs and buildings

Stuntmen used to jump onto pads that were resting on boards; when we hit, the boards broke, cushioning the impact. Later we started using cardboard boxes, stacked two or three high in a square about twelve feet on a side; there was a rope around them to keep them from spreading out on impact. It worked great. Now we use air bags, which are very soft and high-tech. The technology gets better all the time, but of course the stuntman still has to jump. My own stunts have ranged from portraying an Indian who gets shot off a cliff to taking a 110-foot dive onto an air bag.

Jumping through a glass window

The window is made out of a special material called candy glass, which is mostly sugar. (It's the same glass they use to mold breakaway bottles, which are used in fake fights to hit people over the head.) Whereas real glass breaks into pieces with jagged edges that may cut you badly, candy glass shatters into a million tiny bits. You can take a small piece and crush it between your fingers, and it won't even hurt. A stuntman can dive through a candy-glass window and hardly get a scratch.

Making a large pane of candy glass doesn't work, however, because it will break before it can be mounted in the window. So the special effects crew uses real tempered glass and places little explosive charges around the edges. Just as the stuntman hits the window, they explode it, which shatters it to bits. Timing is everything: If they explode the window after he hits, the glass could knock him out, because it's as hard as a rock. If they explode it too early, he'll be diving through flying pieces of broken glass. This stunt has to be done perfectly.

Movie directors always try to film a scene like this in one take (all at once, without stopping the camera). In fact, they use five or six cameras at the same time, to film from different angles. There are no rehearsals. A stuntman won't actually jump through a window (or roll a car, or fall off a cliff) until the camera is running.

Get Famous People to Answer Your Letters

by Michael Levine

Michael Levine is the author of the best-selling *The Kids' Address Book,* which gives complete, correct addresses for many famous people.

f you're a fan of someone famous, such as a basketball star, an actress, or an astronaut, and want to write them a letter, here are some special secrets to improve your chances of getting an answer back.

DO'S:

Send a photograph of yourself. A famous person receives thousands of look-alike letters, and enclosing a photograph gives yours a human face. Because the celebrity sees you as a real person, it's harder to toss aside your letter unanswered.

Enclose a stamped envelope with your address on it. Famous people get a lot of mail, so making it easy to answer your letter will increase your chances of success. Always write your name and address on photos and on *each* page of the letter, in case they get separated.

Make your letter easy to read. This means using a typewriter (if you can type) or at least printing very neatly with a pen. Don't write in crayon, marker, or even pencil. And leave big margins (borders of white space) around the paper.

Keep it short. If you want an autograph, don't write a three-page letter. The reason? Famous people are busy people, and they may set aside long letters to answer "tomorrow"—but tomorrow never comes.

Make your letter special. If you admire someone, say why. Don't be afraid to flatter a celebrity! And don't be shy about showing your own creativity. You can send a poem or drawing—anything to make your request stand out amid the flood of other letters.

DON'TS:

Don't wrap your package in lots of paper, tape, and string. The celebrity may not have a crowbar on hand. Make it easy to open your package.

Don't ask for money. And don't send money, either.

Never send food. Would *you* eat homemade brownies given to you by a total stranger? It may not be safe. Besides, food can spoil in the time it takes to go through the mail.

Don't send a photocopied form letter. The celebrity will figure that you're writing to lots of famous people, and this won't make him or her feel very special.

Build the Eiffel Tower out of... Toothpicks

by Joe King

Joe King showed his toothpick Eiffel Tower on "The Tonight Show Starring Johnny Carson." It can now be seen at the Ripley's Believe It Or Not! Museum in St. Augustine, Florida, which paid $10,000 for it and displays it in a three-story exhibit hall. Joe King is an associate professor of electrical engineering at the University of the Pacific in Stockton, California.

When I decided to build a big model out of toothpicks, I chose the Eiffel Tower—the famous spire in Paris, France—because I thought it would be cheap and fast to make. Boy, was I wrong! It took 110,000 toothpicks and five years. I spent more than $600 on glue and $250 on toothpicks.

One of my earlier geometric sculptures took "only" 10,000 toothpicks. Pointed on both ends, it was eighteen feet long and extended the full length of the living room and into the bedroom, so you couldn't close the bedroom door anymore. My wife has been very patient in dealing with things like this!

Next, I built a chair with 7,000 toothpicks. It weighs only 4 pounds, but it can hold a ton (2,000 pounds) of weight. I know, because I stacked a ton of bricks on it. The chair is strong because it is designed like a bridge. The secret is triangles. Look at any bridge, and you'll see that the metal beams all form triangles. The triangle is a very strong, stable shape.

You can build anything you like with toothpicks. Let's say you want to build a stool. Besides patience, you'll need:

Toothpicks (naturally). Use round toothpicks made by the Diamond Company. They work because they are all *exactly* the same length, 2¾ inches. Other toothpick brands vary in length, which wouldn't matter much if you were just going to pick your teeth with them. But for this type of project, you want parts that are all the same size.

Glue. Use Duco brand household cement, the same stuff you use to mend a broken dish or make model airplanes. It flows slowly, so you can squeeze out a neat line, and it dries as hard as a rock. (Be sure to open the windows and let in lots of fresh air, because the fumes are strong.)

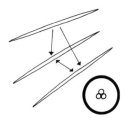

Triple beam

Board. I use a wooden drafting table about 26 inches wide. Draw straight lines all the way across the board from left to right, leaving a space of 2 inches between them. Then glue a permanent row of toothpicks end to end along each of these lines. Later, when you lay out rows of toothpicks to glue together for a project, they will rest against these "stopper rows" and line up nice and straight.

The basic building unit is what I call a "triple beam." It is made by gluing three rows of toothpicks into a single unit. For a stool, you'll make beams that are 18 inches long. First, lay out a row of toothpicks, end to end. Then place a second row next to them, but overlap each toothpick as shown in the illustration. Run a line of cement along the whole length, gluing the two rows together. When it's dry, slide an ordinary butter knife under the row to break it free of the drafting board. Then turn over the row and squeeze another seam of glue down the back side. Place a third row of toothpicks in the groove formed by the first two rows. Overlap these toothpicks, too, but the other way, as shown. This design insures that wherever the tips of two toothpicks meet, there is always reinforcement because of

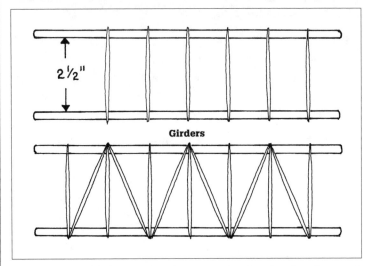

Girders

the overlaps. (If the toothpicks were simply glued end to end, the places where they meet would be weak spots.)

Let's say you want to make a leg for the stool. Place two triple beams on your work board, spaced 2½ inches apart (see illustration above). Lay single toothpicks perpendicular to (across) the two beams. The tips of the toothpicks hang over the beams a little at each end. The distance between the single toothpicks is determined by laying a toothpick diagonally, so it just fits between the two crosspieces. Glue the crosspieces in place. When the glue is dry, go back and snip off the tips of the toothpicks. I use electrical wire snippers, available cheaply at Radio Shack. (Be careful, because the points can take off like rockets. You don't want them to hit you, and if they fall into the carpet, they could stick someone's bare feet!) Finally, glue on the diagonal toothpicks. Let everything dry.

When you have made two of these "girders" (let's call them), you must position them so they stand up from the board, along their long edges, without falling over (see illustration below). To do this, use masking tape. The tape sticks to the board, goes up and over the girder, and sticks to the table on the other side. Do this taping at both ends of each girder. Now glue on crosspieces (see illustration on next page). Let them overlap at each end, and space them out as before by measuring with a diagonal toothpick. Snip the overlapping tips. Then glue the diagonals in place. When everything is dry, you'll have a three-sided beam. Turn it over, and it will be rigid enough to support itself. Glue on crosspieces and diagonals to make the

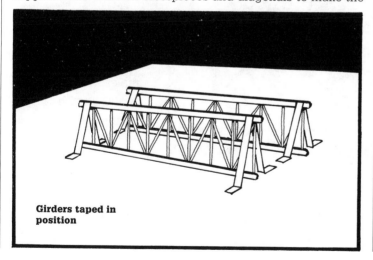

Girders taped in position

fourth side. Snip off the tips. Now you have a 2-inch-square beam that is incredibly strong.

To make it even stronger, glue toothpicks diagonally through the center of the beam at each junction (connection point). They run from one corner to the other. The first toothpick goes one way; the next one along the beam goes crisscross. So each set of two diagonals looks like an X, when viewed from the end of the beam.

This sucker is now so strong that you can jump on it and it won't break. Beams like this are your building blocks. To make the seat, lay out five beams on a flat surface, about 2 inches apart. Connect each beam to the next one with toothpicks laid perpendicularly about 2 inches apart; these are like bridges. Instead of single toothpicks, use two or three together, with a big spot of glue at each end. When these are dry, glue diagonals through the middle of the space

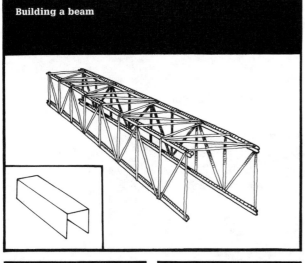

Building a beam

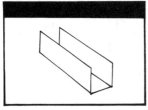

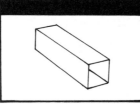

between the beams, from corner to corner. Again, the diagonals alternate, so each pair of two forms a crisscross. Now you have a rigid seat that is 2 inches thick (see illustrations below).

Next, put on the legs, which consist of your standard 2-inch-square beams. All four legs must be the same length, or else the stool will rock. At each corner of the seat, cut out a square notch measuring 2 inches on a side. The tops of the legs will fit into these notches. To attach the legs to the seat, stand two legs up against a wall. Space them apart so they will fit into the notches properly. Make sure they are straight up and down. (You can use a tool called a carpenter's level, if there's one in your house, or just eyeball it.) Stick the two legs to the wall with masking tape. Insert the seat so the legs go into the notches. Use a stack of books to hold up the front end. (The seat should be level with the floor.) Glue the rear legs in place. When the glue is

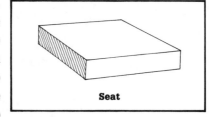

Seat

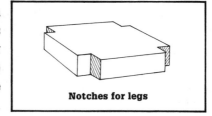

Notches for legs

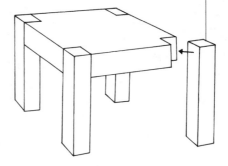

dry, place the remaining two legs into the front notches. Make sure the legs are straight up and down. (You can eyeball them against the rear legs.) Glue them in place.

Now add braces between the legs, like the ones you see on a kitchen chair. Use four of your 2-inch-square beams, cut to the right length to fit. Glue them into place horizontally, about halfway down the legs (see illustration). Finally, use sandpaper or an emery cloth to smooth off all the surfaces of your stool. This gets rid of snags that could catch on your clothes.

Have your friends sit down, and they'll be amazed that such a flimsy looking stool can support their weight!

Now that you have learned the basics, you can use toothpicks to build just about anything. I made a space station that has spokes 4 feet long, with a 35-foot ring hanging out at the ends. (To construct long beams, glue the standard triple beams end to end; you sort of insert them into each other. My Eiffel Tower has beams 10 feet long!)

My next project, by far the biggest I've ever tried, will be the Statue of Liberty. I already have a few gallons of glue stored in my garage…along with a quarter of a million toothpicks!

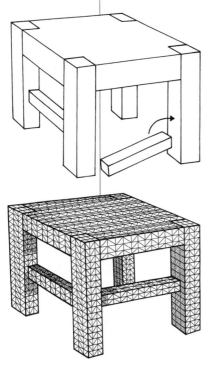

My Thirteen Rules to Live By

by Colin Powell

Over the years I've come upon a number of rules, or thoughts, to live by that can help you with the task of growing up and growing strong.

1. It ain't as bad as you think. It will look better in the morning.
2. Get mad, then get over it.
3. Avoid having your ego so close to your position that when your position falls, your ego goes with it.
4. It can be done!
5. Be careful what you choose. You may get it.
6. Don't let adverse facts stand in the way of a good decision.
7. You can't make someone else's choices. You shouldn't let someone else make yours.
8. Check small things.
9. Share credit.
10. Remain calm. Be kind.
11. Have a vision. Be demanding.
12. Don't take counsel of your fears or naysayers.
13. Perpetual optimism is a force multiplier. (In the military, you always look for ways to increase or multiply your forces.)

General Colin Powell is the former Chairman of the Joint Chiefs of Staff. He led the operations of Desert Storm. General Powell rose from a tough neighborhood in Harlem by hard work and constant study, which he believes are the keys to help anyone climb higher.

How to Twirl a Baton

by Fred Miller

Founder of the United States Twirling Association, Fred Miller served as director of the Blackhawks, a 120-person twirling corps that has won the United States National Championships countless times.

Think back to the last time you saw a baton twirler throw her baton in the air. You probably gasped and crossed your fingers, then sighed with relief when she made the catch. Maybe you'd like to learn the joy of twirling a baton. First, you'll need the right equipment, which means a real baton, not one from the toy store. (You can find a good one through your school band or at a store that sells musical instruments.) A good baton is lightweight and perfectly balanced at the center point. It has a thin shaft, like a golf club. At each end is a piece of rubber. The smaller piece is called the tip; the larger piece is the ball.

A baton should be the right length for *you*. Here's how to measure: Extend your arm straight out and place the tip of the baton against your underarm. The ball should extend slightly beyond your fingertips.

When you practice, don't hold the baton too tightly—this prevents it from twirling. Use a loose, relaxed grip; otherwise, you won't be able to turn your wrist freely. Eventually, you want to have as little continuous contact with your baton as possible. This means being willing to let go of it. Dropping the baton is a natural part of learning. With practice, though, you won't drop it very often.

Wrist twirl

Most people think that baton twirling is done with the fingers, but the main action is in the wrist.

The ball moves along the inside of your arm, and the tip travels along the outside. When the ball and tip return to the starting point, the baton has made one revolution (spin). The pattern is the same for right-hand and left-hand twirls.

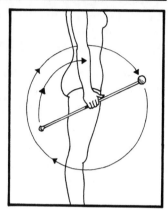

Hold the baton with the ball toward the floor. Your thumb tip points toward the ball.

Turn your wrist so the ball revolves up toward the rear, reaches the top, and then moves toward the front again. Keep turning until the baton returns to the starting position, making one revolution.

Repeat the wrist twirl over and over as smoothly as you can. Don't stop between the end of one twirl and the beginning of the next. As you twist your wrist, be sure the ball moves along

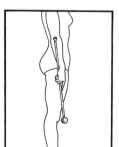
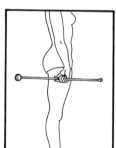
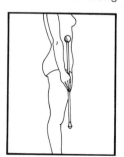

the inside of your arm, while the tip follows a path on the outside of your arm.

In the beginning, your twirls will probably be a little jerky. Remember to keep your fingers loose and relaxed enough for you to twist your wrist. And don't try to increase your speed until you can do sixty continuous twirls smoothly. Eventually, you should be able to complete sixty twirls in one minute.

A right-handed twirler should soon go on to try left-hand twirling. You may have to devote extra practice time to your weaker hand. A twirler's goal is to be ambidextrous—able to do twirls equally well with both hands. Maybe you'll become a twirling champion or a majorette with your school marching band. But even if you just twirl your baton in your backyard, you'll sure learn one thing—it's fun!

Be a Great Punster

by Richard Lederer

Do you like to play with words, turning them round and round and making up jokes? You're not alone. You have a lot of pun pals—including me. All of us know some puns, which are jokes in which one word has two meanings, like this:

Q: What has four wheels and flies?

A: A garbage truck.

This pun comes from the double meaning of the word "flies" —as in "moves through the air" and "winged insects." Here's another:

Q: What kind of shoes are made from banana skins?

A: Slippers.

Nearly every word has more than one sense. And new meanings are being added all the time. For instance, now that computers are part of daily life, old words like "menu" and "window" have new twists. A mouse isn't just a furry little animal anymore; it's also a gray box that scurries around the desk near the computer and has a wire for a tail.

If you want to use puns, just follow these simple rules:

1. Making a pun doesn't excuse bad taste, racism, and offensive gestures.

2. Don't overdo it. Some people can't bear to hear a pun drop. They groan. You'll get a better response from the kind of person who enjoys a joke "just for the pun of it."

3. Keep it simple. A pun should be short and right to the point. Here's a good illustration: "Did you hear about the suc-

Richard Lederer has been elected Punster of the Year by the International Save the Pun Foundation and is the best-selling author of *Get Thee to a Punnery, The Miracle of Language,* and *Anguished English.* He is also a language commentator on National Public Radio.

cessful perfume manufacturer? His business made a lot of scents." It's amazing that this pun has *three* meanings in one space—"scents," "cents," and "sense."

English is the most punderful language on earth, partly because of its huge stock of words—about 616,000 of them, or three and a half times more than any other language. That's a lot of words to make puns with. Our language also has a lot of homophones—words that sound the same but are spelled differently and have different meanings. To celebrate this advantage of English, I once wrote a poem that began: "One night a knight on a hoarse horse rode out upon a road…" As you can see, our language lends itself to making puns.

Here's one of my favorites:

Two ropes walk into a soda fountain, and one rope sits down on a stool. The man behind the counter growls: "Are you one of them ropes?"

"Well, yes…I am," says the first rope.

The man snarls, "Well, we don't serve your kind!" And he takes the rope, twirls it around his head, and tosses it out into the street.

The second rope gets a little worried and thinks, "I'd better disguise myself." So he winds himself into a circle and ruffles up his ends and sits on the stool.

The man behind the counter looks at him suspiciously and says, "Are you one of them ropes?"

The second rope answers, "No, I'm a frayed knot."

You understand puns now, so I don't have to explain that the last sentence is a play on the words "I'm afraid not."

You'll get better and better with language all your life, as long as the marbles stay in your head! If you want to be good at punning, read a lot and build up your vocabulary—then you'll have lots of choices when you look for the right pun word. I hope you'll love making up puns. Everyone can enjoy them, and as the old expression goes, "Time flies when you're having fun."

Or, as one frog said to another, "Time's fun when you're having flies."

Spoonerisms

A "spoonerism" is an accidental reversal of word sounds, such as "Let me sew you to your sheet" for "Let me show you to your seat." The term for this tangled talk honors William A. Spooner, an English clergyman whose slips of the tongue were legendary. Among his more colorful bungles: "a half-warmed fish" for "a half-formed wish"; "parrots and keys" for "carrots and peas"; and "our queer dean" for "our dear queen." You might say that William Spooner set out to be a bird watcher, but instead ended up as a word botcher.

The year 1994 marks the 150th anniversary of his birth, and today people make up spoonerisms on purpose—like the one about the boy who liked English muffins because they had a lot of "crooks and nannies."

You can make them up, too!

Knock-Knock Joke Quiz

We all know some knock-knock jokes, which may be the first truly American humor formula. The jokester says, "Knock, knock." The second person replies, "Who's there?" The knock-knocker comes back with something like "Dwayne." "Dwayne who?" is the ritual response. Then the punch line comes, with a preposterous pun such as "Dwayne the bathtub; I'm dwowning."

Here's a quiz that plays upon people's names. Match each name in the list below with the appropriate ending that follows. The answers are at the end.

Knock, knock. Who's there?

Adelle	Eisenhower	José	Sam and Janet
Amos	Freda	Keith	Sarah
Andy	Harry	Lionel	Sherwood
Arthur	Henrietta	Nicholas	Tarzan
Barry	Humphrey	Oliver	Theresa
Ben Hur	Ira	Osborn	Walter
Della	Isabel	Oswald	Wayne
Desdemona	Isadore	Phillip	Wendy
Dexter	Ivan	Raleigh	Yoda

(Name) who?

1. _____ can you see?

2. _____ big dinner and got sick.

3. _____ dwops keep falling on my head.

4. _____ stripes forever.

5. _____ my bubble gum.

6. _____ catessen.

7. _____ is what a farmer lives in.

8. _____ 'round the flag boys.

9. _____ locked?

10. _____ half as much as a dime.

11. _____ in the USA.

12. _____ quito bit me.

13. _____ bit me again.

14. _____ to be alone.

15. _____ wall carpeting.

16. _____ moon comes over the mountain.

17. _____ halls with boughs of holly.

18. _____ roar if you don't feed it.

19. _____ like a cold drink.

20. _____ me not on the lone prairie.

21. _____ prisoners.

22. _____ the tub so I can take a bath.

23. _____ green, except in winter.

24. _____ an hour, and she hasn't shown up.

25. _____ up, we're late.

26. _____ troubles will soon be over.

27. _____ late for work.

28. _____ doctor in the house?

29. _____ mometer is broken.

30. _____ member Mama.

31. _____ out of order?

32. _____ Lisa hanging on the wall.

33. _____ ever blowing bubbles.

34. _____ evening, you may see a stranger.

35. _____ me, pleath.

36. _____ best knock-knock jokester I've met.

Build a Sandcastle City

by Gerry Kirk

I live at the beach in California, and that's where I started making sandcastles. Later I got interested in sand sculpting as an art form. Now I do huge projects—from life-size dinosaurs to a 48,000-ton model of the lost city of Atlantis. Sometimes I need bulldozers, cranes, and as many as two thousand helpers. But the only materials I use are water and sand. With my methods, you can create sculptures at the beach or in your own backyard sandpile.

Gerry Kirk set the Guinness record for the world's tallest sand sculpture (17.12 meters) with a fantasy castle that he created. His company, Sand Sculptors International, creates sculptures all over the world.

Tools

The basic technique of sand sculpting is to compact sand into big blocks and then carve it with tools. Here's what you'll need:

Sand: The best kind is fairly clean, with grains that are uniform in size. (If the sand grains are all different sizes, touching them with your tools will knock holes in your sculpture.) In the event you have your material delivered, order unwashed masonry sand that has been shaken through a screen so the grains are of uniform size.

Shovels: You'll need a couple of shovels for moving sand and loading it into the forms.

Casting forms: To make big blocks, get a 32-gallon plastic trash can, turn it upside down, and cut out the bottom to form a tapered tube. For making smaller shapes, use white PVC tubes of different sizes up to twelve inches across; cut them into four-

teen-inch lengths. (You can get these supplies at a hardware store.)

Carving tools: I use a metal cooking spatula about three-quarters of an inch wide, along with palette knives sold at art supply stores (be sure they're stiff, and get one small enough to carve little details like eyeballs). I also like square-ended "margin trowels" (one to two inches wide) used by masons. But you don't necessarily have to buy tools; you can use anything that's handy — spoons, popsicle sticks, pieces of plastic that bend into different shapes. As you work with each tool, you'll learn what it can do.

Cheap plastic spray bottle: Spraying water on your sculpture will prevent the sand from drying out and blowing away.

Setting solution: If you want a finished sculpture to remain standing for a while, spray it with a mixture of water and white glue, like Elmer's. Into your bottle pour nine parts of water for every one part of glue. Shake up the mixture, and lightly spray the surface of your work.

Casting

The more tightly you pack the sand into your casting forms, the easier it will be to carve and the longer it will stand up. Turn your bottomless trash can upside down and shovel in some sand, then add a little water. To pack the sand firmly, get inside and stomp. Add more sand and water, and stomp again. Repeat this, layer after layer, until the trash can is filled to the top. Now take two shovels, place the blades under the lip of the trash can, and pry up evenly. The trash can will slide up and off, leaving a cone-shaped block of sand.

To cast in a PVC tube, place the sand and water inside and pack it firmly with the handle of your margin trowel or other tool. Then use the tool to tap the sides of the tube; that will loosen it, and pretty soon you'll be able to slide the tube right off. The sand will be the perfect shape for carving a tower on a castle.

Carving

First, let's carve a simple roof, like that on a barn.

1. Start with a rectangular block of sand. (Either trim the cone you made in the trash can, or use a rectangular casting form.)

2. Look down at the top of the block, and you'll see a rectangle. Draw a line down the center of it, the long way. (Scratch the line with the corner of a spatula.) This represents the "ridge line," which is the highest peak of the roof. Starting at either of the two long edges of the block, use a two-inch-wide trowel to shave the sand at whatever angle you want your roof to slant. (In other words, carve from the outside edge toward the middle, angling up toward the ridge line.) Don't try to cut the whole thing in one slice, or you'll put too much pressure on the sand and it could fall apart. Then shave the other side of the roof the same way.

3. Cut the eaves (roof overhangs), which will make your

new roof stick out past the walls. Start on either side, using the edge of a trowel to make a long cut about half an inch deep along the line where the roof meets the wall. Then trim the wall straight down, removing half an inch of sand all the way to the base of your block. This creates an overhanging roof. Carve the other side of the block the same way.

4. Figure out where you want windows. Lightly mark the perimeter (outline) of a window. Then begin carving at the center and work outward toward the edges, which you cut straight and sharp. Carving the windows about one inch deep creates deep shadows that help the windows show up from a distance.

Finishing Touches

Complete your building by adding realistic details. You may want to carve steps leading up to a door, or sand "bushes" where the building meets the ground.

To add a chimney, mark off a three-inch square on the roof, then carve it out to form a notch. Now cast a chimney shape by *tightly* packing sand into a small PVC tube (about two inches across). Gently pull off the tube. Pick up the column of sand carefully, and place one end into the notch. Fill in the notch with more sand, if it's needed, and smooth the area around the base of the chimney. If you want to carve a lip around the top of your chimney, make a shallow cut (like you did to make an eave) and carve straight down to create four sides. You can carve many kinds of chimneys, so look at pictures of houses and castles, then try to duplicate what you see.

To put a round tower on your castle, use a PVC tube to make a cylinder of sand. Looking down at the top of the cylinder, which forms a circle, mark the center point. Carve a cone shape (like an upside-down ice cream cone), working from the bottom up toward the center point. (Do this the same way you shaved the roof on your barn.) Then make a half-inch-deep cut for the eave, and carve the walls downward all the way around the tower to create an overhanging roof. Finish the tower by carving out a gothic window (a narrow arch, with a point at the top) and maybe a spiral staircase somewhere.

With practice you'll be able to sculpt sand easily and fast. (I can carve a tower in the time it takes to tell you about it.) Sand sculpture is fun. And when you go to the beach, you'll really wow people!

The Unavoidable Fate of Sandcastles

When you make things of sand, you have to realize that your works of art won't last. (That is, unless you spray them with a mixture of glue and water.) It's okay. In fact, sometimes I like to watch a sandcastle slowly fall to pieces, which happens as the wind blows away grains of sand, or the tide comes in at the beach. Pretty soon the castle looks as if time has crumbled it and left only picturesque ruins. It's as though the castle has been falling apart for four hundred years—but it's only existed for four hours!

Be sure to take photographs.

Trick Shots at the Pool Table

by Steve Mizerak

Steve Mizerak was four years old when his father first lifted him onto a pool table. He sank the eight ball in the side pocket and has been playing ever since. He won the U.S. Open Straight Pool Tournament four years in a row and the world title three times running. His books include *The Complete Book of Pool*.

It's fun to show off at the pool table by doing trick shots. They look almost impossible, so you'll amaze your friends. I even got my mug on TV doing stunts like these. Trick shots go back to the 1700s, and one old-time character could even make balls jump from table to table! The tricks I'll teach you are easier than that, but you'll still have to practice. So let's rack 'em up!

Bank Deposit

Here's the lazy man's (or woman's) way to rack the balls. To set up this shot, place the point of the wooden triangle on the round spot on the table. (This is the place where you normally rack the balls.) Put fourteen balls into the rack, but leave out the one ball. Rest the point of the triangle on the cue ball, as shown. The one ball is placed on the table to the right of the rack.

Stroke the one ball toward the side cushion of the table. Your cue stick should hit the ball fairly hard, at a point slightly above

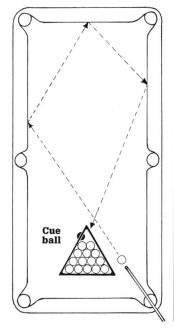

Cue ball

center and to the right. (Pool players call this "high right-hand English.") The ball bounces off the cushion three times. Then it goes into the rack, knocking the cue ball away. The one ball ends up where it belongs, at the point of the triangle, and the rack drops into place around all the balls. Pretty fancy! And this shot isn't especially hard to do.

Neck and Neck

Sink *four* balls in one shot? Sure, why not? To set up this shot, place the cue ball an equal distance from either side cushion.

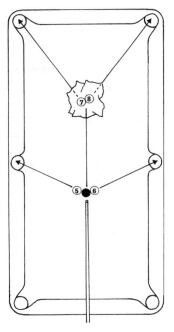

It should be three inches closer to your end of the table than to the opposite end. Place the five ball and the six ball so they're "frozen" to the cue ball, which means they're pressed tightly against it. The balls should be in the positions shown. Now place the seven ball and eight ball on the table, just on your side of the round spot at the far end. The balls should be frozen to each other at the angle shown.

With a smooth, solid stroke, hit the cue ball. If you've set things up properly, the six ball will go in the right side pocket and the five ball in the left side pocket. The seven and eight balls will go in the far corner pockets. You've sunk four balls at once!

A tip: After practicing this shot, you can make it look even more impressive by draping a square handkerchief over the seven and eight balls. When the cue ball hits, the two balls will shoot out from under the hanky. It looks pretty mysterious, and it's guaranteed to prompt oohs and aahs from your friends.

How to Break

Let's say you're playing Eight Ball. In this game one player has to sink all the striped balls and the other has to sink the solid-color balls. Whoever finishes first must then sink the eight ball.

The balls are racked with the eight ball in the middle of the triangle. If you want to play it safe on the break, aim at the head ball (the ball at the point of the triangle facing toward you). Hit this ball straight on. Using this strategy lessens the chance of scratching (hitting the white cue ball into a pocket).

If you want to live a little more dangerously, place the cue ball offset to the left, about halfway between the round mark on the table and the side cushion. (These instructions are for a right-handed player; if you're a lefty, just reverse the sides.) Aim at the ball just to the left of the point of the triangle; in other words, at the second ball to the left. Use a firm, solid stroke. This kind of break gives the balls more action, which improves your chances of sinking one (or more) of them. However, it also makes it easier to scratch in the corner pocket!

Make a Finger Ring from a Dollar Bill

by Patrick Schlagel

Somehow, folding paper is more interesting when you use money instead of blank paper. To make a finger ring, first ask, "Mom, Dad—can I borrow a dollar?" Then follow these instructions.

Magician Patrick Schlagel has been folding paper ever since they started passing it out in school, learning from other students who were equally unwilling to listen to the teacher. He has folded everything from traditional airplanes and water bombs to a stegosaurus and a cuckoo clock—all made entirely out of paper.

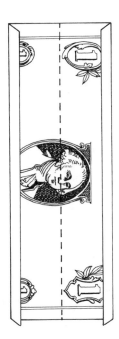

Lay the bill face down on a table and fold the white borders on the long sides of the bill away from you. Turn the bill over. Fold it in half along the dotted line so that the border folds go on the inside.

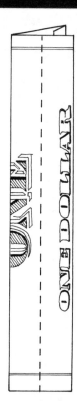

Fold the bill in half again, along the dotted line.

Fold down the white border at the top end, creasing it toward you.

Fold down the top part of the bill so you have a small square (not a rect-angle) with the word "ONE" show-ing.

Now the bill looks like this.

Fold the bottom two inches of the bill upward and away from you. This fold should be next to the O in the large word "ONE" across the back of the bill.

Turn the bill over. Fold it diagonally on the dotted line.

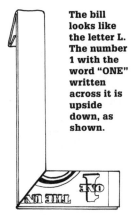

The bill looks like the letter L. The number 1 with the word "ONE" written across it is upside down, as shown.

Turn the bill over. Lay the shorter piece (from A to B) along the first finger of your left hand. The tip of your finger is at B.

Then wrap the longer piece
around the tip of your finger.
The point marked X will
meet Z.

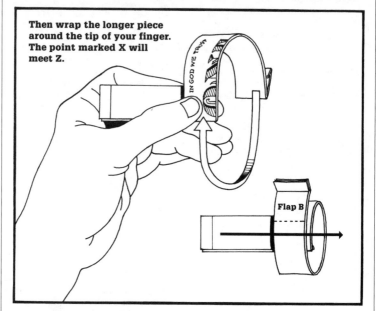

Flap B

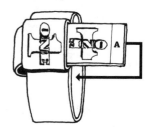

Use your left thumb to hold the
bill in the shape of a circle by
pressing the bill against your
finger. With your right hand
gently pull up flap B, which is
the piece that says "ONE."

Now fold piece A as shown.
Next, fold flap B down over
piece A.

Tuck the white border of flap B
under piece A. Then fold flap A
downward into the ring.

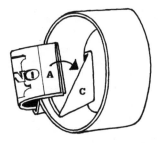

This shows the inside of the ring. Insert flap A into the slanted pocket marked C. (You may have to poke flap A to get it to fit inside the pocket.) Doing this locks the ring so it won't come unfolded.

Put the ring on your finger and show it to your friends. But be prepared— they'll want you to teach them how to make a ring for a dollar, too!

More about Folding Paper

For information on origami (from the Japanese: *ori*, to fold; *kami*, paper), send a stamped, self-addressed envelope to:

Friends of the Origami Center
40-05 166th Street
Flushing, NY 11358

Books on folding money are available at local magic shops or from:
Magic, Inc.
5082 North Lincoln Avenue
Chicago, IL 60625
(312) 334-2855

Make the Most of Your Life

by Ronald Reagan

Ronald Reagan served from 1981 to 1989 as the fortieth president of the United States.

Our school years are a time when we become aware of the wonderful world around us, of the opportunities—and yes, the dangers—it can pose. My young friends, you are so fortunate to live in the greatest country in the world. It may not be perfect, but it is an example and an inspiration for people around the world.

Think of what has happened in Eastern Europe recently. The people there weren't allowed to do what you and I take for granted. They could not go to the church or synagogue of their choice, couldn't read a newspaper of their choice, couldn't choose their job, couldn't travel as they wanted. And they never knew whether their neighbor was a true friend or a spy for the government. When they went to the grocery store, there often was no food. And they didn't have a real choice when they went to the voting booth, either. In short, they had no real control over their own lives. In the United States we can't imagine such a way of living.

Yet they kept hoping and praying for change. They begged their leaders for reform, but the leaders wouldn't listen, and so the people took to the streets. Now they are taking back control of their lives and their countries. And do you know what they say when they're asked what they want their country to be like? They say they want it to be more like America.

That is because we have a free enterprise system. We are free to pursue our dreams and goals, free from government getting in the way, free to live our lives as we want. That doesn't happen under socialism and communism. Life in our great country is a wonderful adventure, and we never know where it will take us.

Look at me, for example. I started out in a small town in Illinois. I played football in high school. And part of what makes football great is that it doesn't matter if you're rich or poor, if you're black or white, or where you live — there is an opportunity for each of us to succeed. You can be doctors, nurses, lawyers, teachers, athletes, astronauts, firefighters, actors, even presidents. In America, everyone has a chance.

In my own case, after college I became a radio sports announcer for baseball and football games. Next, I went to Hollywood and got a job as a movie actor. All of a sudden, it seemed, I was running for governor of California; I never thought I'd win, but I did. Before I knew it, I was on my way to the White House for eight years.

And now here I am, out of work!

As you build your own lives, remember that there are so many people who want to help you make it — your friends, your families, your teachers, and of course members of the business community. But you must do your part, too. Study hard in school. Be kind to your neighbors. Respect your parents. And please, stay away from drugs. Drugs can take the brightest hopes and destroy them, and I don't want that to happen. We need you!

Your whole life is ahead of you. I know it will be great!

How to Do a "360" on a Surfboard

by Rob Machado

Rob Machado won his first contest at the age of twelve in the United States Amateur Surfing Champion-ships. He went on to victory in the Ocean Pacific junior division contest at Hun-tington Beach and even took first place in a profes-sional contest while he was still an amateur. In his first year as a pro he won two con-tests sponsored by the Professional Surfing Associa-tion of America.

 breaking wave is so beautiful and graceful. My goal in surfing is to be one with it — to look like I should be on that wave. I don't think I'm quite there yet, but I try to be styl-ish, and I also like to do maneuvers like 360s. Turning your surf-board around in a complete circle while you're riding a wave is called a 360. You have to pick the right wave, one that's slow and crumbly and not curling. (If you try a 360 on a powerful wave that's hollow, like the ones in Hawaii, you'll run into di-saster because it will break on you.) Pick a weaker wave, and take off on it. The front of your body should be facing the wave. (In my case, since I surf with my right foot forward, I'd be go-ing to my left.)

The secret of doing a 360 is to get the fins on your surfboard completely out of the water. That's the only way the board can turn around. (The kind of board I ride, called a thruster, has three fins.) To do the maneuver, you will make a weight adjust-ment on your board. Shift your weight onto your front foot, and at the same time make a quick little turn up the face of the wave. This will break your fins out of the water. Now your board is aiming straight up the wave. Your fins are pointing down the wave toward the beach and your body is facing out to sea. The back of the board has started spinning in a circle.

Next shift your weight onto your back foot, which will force your fins into the water again. When the fins catch in the wave, you will complete the circle. Now you are back where you started, and you just keep riding! At surfing contests the crowds love to see 360s, so if anyone's watching you, they're probably cheering.

Doing an Aerial

These days surfers use speed to do radical maneuvers on a wave. To do an aerial, you race up the face of the wave, hit the curl, and actually release out of the water—and then land successfully on the wave again. You and your board both leave the water, so it's definitely one of the hardest maneuvers.

To do it you need a fast wave with "a lot of face"—one that has an open face (not a hollow curl) and a long slope. It's the kind of wave you see at Malibu. To get up speed, you do what's called S-turning, going up and down the wave continually. (With a thruster it's fairly easy to gain speed by S-turning.) The ideal place on the wave to do an aerial is where it's just beginning to break and there's a little foam. You'll use that white water almost as a launch pad.

You go very fast up to the wave's peak and just keep going. Now you're in the air above the breaking wave. Most people leave the water about six inches or a foot, but some have gotten a lot higher. The higher you get, of course, the harder it is to land. The tough part is keeping your surfboard underneath you. It's a matter of balance and control, which takes a lot of practice.

Once you're in the air, point the board down so you're looking at the face of the wave. You've just got to hope that your landing area will be a good one. You don't have any control over it—the wave is going to break the way it's going to break. I guess that's what makes surfing so neat. And suddenly you're back in the water, riding the wave again!

Thoughts on Being a Stand-up Comic

by Jerry Seinfeld

Jerry Seinfeld, the star and writer of the hit TV series "Seinfeld," is also one of the busiest stand-up comics today. He has won American Comedy Awards for Funniest Male Stand-up Comic and for Best Actor in a Comedy Series.

 became fascinated by comedians at the age of eight, watching them on television. I remember my parents telling me, "This man's job is to come out and be funny for people." I couldn't believe it. "That's his whole job?" I asked. "Are you kidding me?" And they said, "No, he's kidding us."

I knew I was going to be a comedian at a very young age. I remember one time I made a friend laugh so hard that he sprayed a mouthful of cookies and milk all over me, and I liked it. That was the beginning.

The stage to me is not a pulpit. In my act, I don't like to mix politics and comedy. It's not funny to say, "I'm upset." It may be provocative or interesting, but that's not what comedy is about. To me, comedy is about getting upset at the *wrong* thing.

Also, I always like to leave the stage a little early. I'm a true minimalist.

Find Your Way Anywhere Using Only the Sun and Your Wristwatch

by Merry Vaughan

Let's say you don't know where you are. (This describes me most of the time!) You're on a hike, or even a walk across town, and you've gotten turned around. You feel lost. If you can reckon which direction is south, you're saved, because then you can also figure out north, east, and west.

Merry Vaughan is a former zookeeper who learned this trick from a friend and thought it was pretty neat.

All you need is a watch and a thin, straight twig (or a pencil, a tightly rolled dollar bill, or anything you can think of). Lay your watch faceup on the ground. Be sure it's in the sunshine. Hold the twig so it's straight up and down, and position it above the pointed end of the hour hand. The twig casts a shadow on the watch. Now rotate the watch until the shadow falls across the center point of the watch face (the place where the hands are

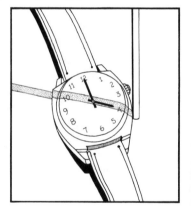

attached). Here's the rule to figure out which direction is south: It lies exactly halfway between the hour hand and twelve o'clock.

For example, let's say the time is four o'clock in the afternoon. Position the twig at the end of the hour hand, and rotate the watch until the twig's shadow falls across the center point.

South would be halfway between twelve o'clock and four
o'clock—that is, at two o'clock.
North is in exactly the opposite direction (at eight o'clock).
Now that you know south and
north, you can also figure out
which ways are east and west.

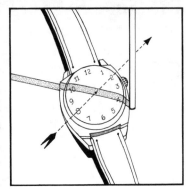

With this system, you'll always know where you're going.

Look Great on Ice Skates

by Peggy Fleming

The key to my ice skating technique is my background in ballet. Ballet teaches you to center your body. For example, you learn to keep your hips square. That way, when you do a jump or raise your leg on skates, you won't be as likely to open out your hip to get your leg up higher. This keeps your weight centered, so you feel balanced.

Another secret is to "skate in your knees," which means to have a limber, springy sort of feeling in them. If your knees are stiff, you can't extend your legs very far as you skate. Picture a rower in a boat: If he makes a short stroke with the oars, he won't go as fast as when he takes a long stroke and pulls with real strength.

Also be sure to have good posture and good carriage. A trick here is to hold in your stomach, which makes your back straighten up. Whether or not you become a champion skater, this is a good rule to practice for life. If you slouch, your body doesn't work as well as it should; you can't get enough air in your lungs. Having good posture opens up your body, so you get more oxygen. It also keeps you in good position so you don't get injured by being off balance.

Try to make your glide over the ice look quiet and effortless. You don't have to flail your arms and sweat like a hockey player to gather speed. It's possible to do it very gracefully and subtly by using crossovers. (A crossover is the skating stroke where one foot crosses over the other and then pushes off.) You

Peggy Fleming won the gold medal in figure skating at the 1968 Winter Olympics, as well as many national and world championships. Her artistic style has set a standard by which figure skaters continue to be judged.

have to feel it; it's a mind-over-matter thing. With three or four crossovers you can go from a standstill to full speed! That adds a lot of excitement and emotion to your performance. It looks effortless, and that's the whole idea. People won't know how you did it. Doing simple moves with power underneath is what makes you better than other skaters.

Having this good basic technique will carry you through. It's been my secret for as long as I've been performing as an athlete.

Arrange Flowers Beautifully

by Martha Stewart

I think flowers look prettiest when they look natural, as if they were growing in a well-tended garden, not just stuck in a container. Here are some ideas for making beautiful flower arrangements.

Martha Stewart writes books that explain how to do all kinds of things for gracious living. She lives in Connecticut, where she grows lots of flowers to arrange.

Picking

If you have a garden, pick flowers before ten o'clock in the morning. By high noon they'll be very soft and ready to wilt, but in the morning the flowers are still cool from the night. If you want fully opened flowers, pick those. But if you want flowers that will unfurl, pick buds. (However, don't pick some buds and some open flowers, because in your arrangement some will soon be sagging while others are just opening up.)

Cut the flowers with long enough stems for whatever container you imagine using. Use very sharp garden clippers, and cut the stems at an angle, because that leaves the plant looking nicer. Be sure not to bruise or bash the flowers when you pick them. Treat them gently.

Arranging

Carry the flowers inside and lay them flat. Strip off the excess leaves on the stems—you don't want foliage going in the water. Immediately place the flowers in room-temperature water. (Cold or warm water might shock them.) Now decide what kind of arrangement you want to make, and pick a container your mom would like you to use. It could be a vase, an old bottle, or a basket with a plastic liner (like a quart container from the delicatessen).

A great idea is to use a whole row of tiny glasses, like juice glasses. Fill them with water and choose your blossoms one by one. Big roses or poppies work well. Cut the stems short enough so they just sit, one perfect flower per glass. Then arrange the glasses in a row down the center of a table. This looks very pretty.

If you're going to make a big arrangement in a vase, start with the largest flowers. Keep these stems shorter. Then start putting in smaller flowers, keeping their stems a little longer. They'll be a background for the bigger blossoms.

My prize secret? Don't skimp. Use *lots* of flowers in a big arrangement. You don't want flowers moving around loose in the neck of a vase. You want them to be crowded—a huge profusion of blossoms!

A Tip or Two

If your flowers have gummy stems, like carnations or snapdragons, put a teaspoon of Clorox bleach in the water so they don't turn the water green. To keep flowers perky, put a little plant food in the water.

Win Big at Monopoly

by Philip Orbanes

Monopoly is like life. There are no hard and fast rules for success. But there are principles that improve your chances. If you learn them, you'll win more than you lose.

Have no mercy. Remember that the object of the game is to bankrupt (wipe out) all the other players. Do everything you can to make them lose their money and property. Never let an opponent off easy. Luck plays a big part in the game, and luck can turn against you if you don't bankrupt a player as quickly as you can.

Know the equipment. The game has thirty-two houses and sixteen hotels. Knowing this can help you create housing shortages (see below). There are sixteen Chance cards, which will most likely send you to another space, and sixteen Community Chest cards, which will most likely give you a reward. (Tip: By keeping track of the cards played, you can figure out which ones haven't come up yet.)

Learn the chances of rolling different numbers with the dice. Seven is the most common roll; then 6 and 8; then 5 and 9; then 4 and 10; then 3 and 11. The least common numbers are 2 and 12.

Know when to stay in Jail. Pay $50 to get out of Jail if it's early in the game, when lots of properties are still unowned and undeveloped. You want to be in motion around the board to

Philip Orbanes has been inventing since he was eight. As an executive at Parker Brothers, he led the company into video games and developed many NERF toys.

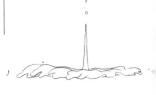

buy up property. But if most properties are developed between Jail and the Go to Jail space, roll the dice and hope you stay in Jail. It's better than paying rent! This rule is very important when certain dangerous color groups, such as the oranges, are heavily developed.

Always buy an unowned property if:
- no other player owns a property in its color group (orange, red, purple, etc.)
- it gives you a second or third property of its group
- it blocks an opponent from getting a monopoly
- it is an orange property. The oranges are an excellent color group. They're not very expensive to buy and develop, they are landed on often, and they can knock out an unlucky player who has to pay you rent.

Exceptions: You don't need to buy one of a group if two other players each have a property of the group, and also have more valuable groups split between them. Example: Players A and B own all the reds and oranges between them. They each own a light purple. You land on the unowned light purple. You don't need to buy it. Counter-example: Players A and B own all the oranges and light purples between them. They each own a red. You land on the unowned red. You *should* buy it. Otherwise, you increase the chances that these players will make a trade and develop the most powerful monopoly of these three groups—the reds.

Know when and where to build. Putting up houses and

hotels makes it easier for you to bankrupt the other players. That's why many players build all they can afford. But this strategy leads to losses when houses must be "torn down" to pay rents or other penalties. You should build:

- when you form the first monopoly
- if you'll still have enough cash left to pay likely expenses, such as rents on Railroads or Utilities, Luxury Tax, and the nasty Community Chest or Chance cards that haven't come up yet. Keep $200 in cash if there are no other monopolies against you, but $400 if there are one or more monopolies.

Here are some basic principles of building:

1. Build a monopoly up to at least three houses per property before you start building on a second monopoly. (Rents rise a *lot* once a third house is added to a property.)

2. If you can afford an extra house, put it on the most expensive property of the monopoly.

3. Build up to the fourth house or hotel level only if you have plenty of cash to spare. (This is true *unless* the group is one of the first three on the board — dark purple, light blue, or light purple. Due to the low rents of these groups, you *should* try to build hotels here.)

4. Try to develop a low-rent monopoly early in the game. You want to bankrupt the other players before they can develop "heavier" monopolies against you.

Know when to cause a "housing shortage." If you own only low-rent monopolies, quickly build three or four houses per property. This limits the number available to owners of high-rent monopolies, because the bank will have a "housing shortage."

Never move up to a hotel if the houses you return to the bank would let an opponent develop an expensive monopoly. Example: the yellow monopoly has just been formed. There are only three houses in the bank, but six hotels. You own the light blue group with four houses each. Do *not* buy hotels. Doing so

Fun Facts about Monopoly

Money, money, money. Parker Brothers prints about 50 billion dollars' worth of Monopoly money each year. That's more than twice the amount of real money made by the U.S. Mint.

Monopoly boards smuggled into prisoner-of-war camps during World War II contained hidden escape maps. Packs of Monopoly money concealed real money for use by escaping American prisoners.

About 100 million Monopoly sets have been sold around the world.

Solid gold playing pieces were part of the most expensive Monopoly set ever made. A creation of the Dunhill company, it was worth $25,000.

Monopoly sets are made in many languages, including Italian, Greek, Spanish, Japanese, and many others. Boardwalk is called Rue de la Paix (France), Schlossalle (Germany), Kalverstrat (Holland), and Mayfair (England).

Records for the longest game played: In a bathtub, 99 hours; underwater, 45 days; upside down, 36 hours.

would give the player owning the yellows a chance to build up to hotels on them.

Know how to get the most out of mortgaging. To raise money when you need it, you'll have to mortgage properties. Here are some guidelines:

1. Mortgage single properties first. Try *not* to mortgage a deed from a group where you own two or more properties. (You can't build on a color group if one of its properties is mortgaged.)

2. Mortgage single properties if the cash raised helps you develop a monopoly up to at least three houses per property (or up to hotels on the light blues or either purple group.)

3. When you have a choice, mortgage your properties in this order:

a) Colored properties closest to GO

b) A single Utility

c) Railroads

d) The Utility monopoly (you want to keep Utilities because they produce a lot of cash, which you'll need to unmortgage properties!)

4. Don't mortgage Illinois, New York, or Boardwalk if you can avoid it. These properties have higher chances of getting landed on than many other properties.

5. Pay off mortages only if you have developed your monopolies to at least three houses per property, and only if you can afford it.

6. Pay off mortgages in the reverse order in which you mortgaged them (*unless* you can develop a new, unmortgaged monopoly by doing otherwise.)

Keep track of the money in the game. Each player starts with $1,500. On one trip around the board, he makes an average of $170 if no houses have been bought yet. (This takes into account passing GO, earning rewards, paying rents, and so on.) If you know how much money another player has, you are able to figure out how high he'll bid if a property is auctioned off, or how many houses/hotels he can buy without mortgaging his property.

Know how to trade. The rules allow you to trade with other players during the game. To make trades that give you the most benefit, follow these principles:

1. Early in the game, trade to get low-cost properties that produce a steady income—namely the Railroads or Utilities.

2. Try to trade for a monopoly that can dominate the board quickly, like the light purples, oranges, or reds.

3. When trading developable properties, try to trade for those of equal or greater value and those that lie closer to Free Parking.

4. Make a trade only if it will improve your chances of winning. Don't let another player persuade you to trade just for the sake of trading.

5. When you interest an opponent in a trade, let him do

most of the suggesting. You may get more than you expected.

Be the kind of player others won't mind losing to. Be polite, knowledgeable, and considerate (instead of being insulting, a know-it-all, or a browbeater). Monopoly usually can't be won without gaining the cooperation of other players. If you don't show reasonable goodwill toward your opponents, you'll have a tough time making beneficial trades or financial deals.

Study these rules, then give them a try. You'll be rolling in Monopoly money before you know it!

Want to Play in a Monopoly Tournament?

Organizations around the country hold local Monopoly tournaments— the first step toward crowning the next world champion. If you want to enter a local competition, write to:

Monopoly Tournament Director
Parker Brothers
50 Dunham Road
Beverly, MA 01915

How to Pan for Gold

by Michael Orelove

Michael Orelove, an Alaska State Gold Panning Champion, has won so many gold-panning trophies with his brother, Joel, that he has a special trophy room in his house to display them. He has taught thousands of visitors to Alaska the secrets of panning for gold.

The secret to panning for gold is not in the size of the pan or in the way you shake it—it's all in your mind. The secret is, THINK GOLD.

You are trying to find all the gold that's buried in the ground. Gold is heavy—heavier than dirt, sand, gravel, and rocks. And heavy things sink to the bottom. It's the law of gravity.

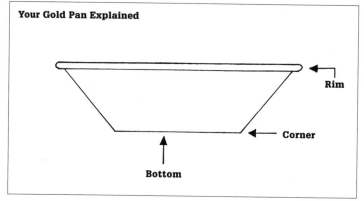

Your Gold Pan Explained

Rim

Corner

Bottom

Put some dirt in your pan and follow these three easy steps to wealth and happiness.

Step 1: Add water to your pan and shake. Use lots of water. Shake the pan vigorously so that the water and dirt make a very loose mixture of slush. Don't spill any of the dirt out of the pan. Remember, gold is heavy, so if you have a loose blend of slush, the heavy elements will sink to the bottom of the pan. That's gravity working for you. And THINK GOLD.

Some people like to shake the pan with a side-to-side motion. Others prefer a front-to-back motion. Some people like to use a circular motion and make small whirlpools in the pan. I have often seen people shake their entire body and do a "gold dance." All of these methods work. The object is to get a loose mixture of the dirt and water so that the heavy matter will sink.

As you are shaking, tilt the pan at a slight angle so that a

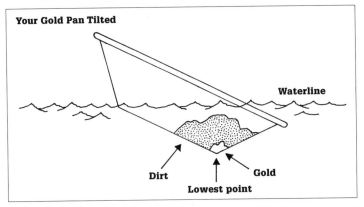

Your Gold Pan Tilted

Waterline

Dirt   **Gold**

Lowest point

portion of the bottom area is the lowest spot. The bottom round edge is known as the "corner" of the pan. It's hard to imagine that a round pan can have a corner, but prospectors are an unusual lot. Keep shaking the pan until all the heavy elements work their way down to the bottom corner. Don't spill any dirt out.

How do you know when the gold is at the bottom? If you are thinking gold, you can almost see it moving through the dirt. Sometimes you can hear it. Once I even smelled it!

Step 2: Now that you have all the heavy stuff at the bottom, what's left at the top? The light stuff, of course. Now start washing this away one layer at a time, just as if you were peeling an onion.

Keeping the pan tilted at an angle, dip it in and out of the water. Do not shake—just dip it in and out. When you pull the pan out of the water, a small layer of dirt on top will float away. By varying the tilt of the pan, you can control how much dirt you wash out.

Do not spill the dirt out of the pan. If you do, you will be spilling out the entire contents, including the elements at the bottom. By dipping, you are washing away only the top layer. The matter at the bottom should remain there until you uncover it.

Keep dipping until you have most of the dirt washed away. When you are near the bottom, remove the pan from the water, leaving a small amount of water in the pan. With a circular motion, slowly swirl away the remaining water to uncover the sediment on the bottom.

Note: It is customary to shout "GOLD!" when you find it, but not too loud, as there may be some claim jumpers nearby.

Step 3: Celebrate! It is also customary to share some of your nuggets with the prospector who taught you how to pan for gold. You can usually find me at Last Chance Basin or Gold Creek in Juneau, Alaska. I'm the one with the biggest pan in town.

Walking on the Moon
by Buzz Aldrin

Maybe someday we'll take vacations on the moon. I hope so. In 1969 I was lucky enough to make the first trip to the moon, heading into space in a capsule atop a *Saturn V* rocket as tall as a 35-story building. The booster had the power of an atomic bomb, and after the third stage roared to life, we were moving 25,000 miles an hour. That really is "faster than a speeding bullet," as Superman says.

In space there isn't any gravity. Aboard the spacecraft we slept on couches with loose nets around them so we wouldn't float around. The food wasn't bad at all (we even had little hot dogs), but most things had to be sticky so they wouldn't separate. Peas served in space must be mixed with a cream sauce, or else you have a cabin full of floating peas.

After traveling a quarter of a million miles, we reached orbit around the moon. Astronaut Michael Collins manned the command module, while Neil Armstrong and I landed the lunar module on the moon's surface. The gravity there is only one-sixth of Earth's pull, and I had fun finding out what it's like to move around. You can hop like a kangaroo!

On Earth if you lose your balance, you have to recover very fast. But not on the moon. If you stumble, you have lots of time to get your feet back underneath you again.

The nicest part about being on the moon is that you feel very free. You can move in fun ways that are impossible on Earth. I hope *you* get to the moon one day and try it for yourself.

Dr. Buzz Aldrin, a member of the *Apollo 11* mission, was the second person in human history to set foot on the moon. He is now a space exploration consultant and futurist.

Name and Title Index

Subject Index

Thanks!

A tip of the Hatlo hat to Chris Holmes, who first suggested I write a kids' version of my adult book, *Tricks of the Trade.* The Hanstad family made the same suggestion and contributed ideas. Tom, Peter, Charlie, and Judy Munzig came up with great suggestions, as did Ben Marks of *Sunset* magazine, Dr. Jim Halverson, Jim Buckley, and Barnaby Conrad. Many thanks also to my esteemed editors, Marnie Patterson and Alan Andres, to manuscript editor Dorothy Henderson, and to designer Catharyn Tivy.

David Zaboski drew the wonderful flip book that is part of *Tricks of the Trade for Kids.* Victor Paredes did the very fine instructional illustrations. Alice Martell, agent extraordinaire, handled all business matters with efficiency and a smile.

My wife, Merry, improved the book vastly with her editorial wit and wisdom. When there's a lot of work to be done, Merry sometimes flops down on the couch and jokes, "Shall I just sit here…and look pretty?" She always does (look pretty, I mean).